BIOLOGY

IN
THE WORLD
OF
THE FUTURE

BIOLOGY

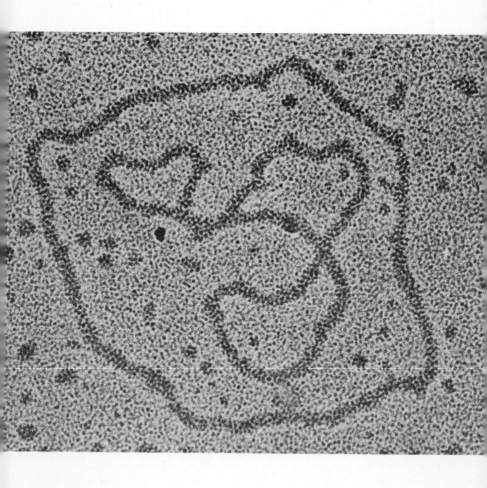

IN

THE WORLD

OF

THE FUTURE

BY

HAL HELLMAN

PUBLISHED BY

M. Evans and Company, Inc. NEW YORK

AND DISTRIBUTED IN ASSOCIATION WITH

J. B. Lippincott Company

PHILADELPHIA AND NEW YORK

For Sheila, Mort, Perri, David, Judy and Bingo.

ACKNOWLEDGEMENTS:

The author wishes to thank Joseph N. Muzio, Associate Professor of Biology, Kingsborough Community College of the City University of New York, who reviewed the entire manuscript, and Dr. I. Bernard Weinstein, Associate Professor of Medicine, College of Physicians and Surgeons of Columbia University, who reviewed portions of it. Their comments and suggestions were very helpful.

Contents

Prologue

THE JUDGE LOOKED down at the unhappy man standing before him, but spoke for the record. He said gently, "I am convinced that John Clarkson Martin has changed sufficiently that it would not be fair to expect him to continue bearing the burdens of his past familial and vocational life. This has come about as a direct result of his having contracted a most unusual illness, and subsequent organ transplants and biochemical and psychotherapeutical treatment not of his own accord.

"I therefore declare that the said John Martin, of 101 Jackson Place, District A22, Northwest Region, no longer exists. His place will be taken by John Clarkson Mercer, whose new address is 1335 Grant Avenue in the same district.

"The state will see to it that vocational counseling and training are given to Mr. Mercer so that he may take up a career more in keeping with his new personality and physical characteristics. It is hoped that Mr. Mercer will be able to re-establish favorable relationships with his wife and children. If not, the state will continue to provide support to them for as long as is necessary."

The new Mr. Mercer said, "Thank you, Your Honor," glanced briefly over at a tearful wife and three of the six other people with whom he shared an apartment, and left the courtroom.

Judge Andrew Mann, only 257 years old and hence a relatively young man, was nevertheless old enough to be able to remember a time when there were no such cases. Life was much simpler then. But there was no question that when several of a man's major organs have been transplanted, and he has taken the necessary drugs, hormones, and so on, his body biochemistry does tend to change. It seemed very clear too that this has a strong effect on his brain, bringing about personality and mental differences as well. In effect, he may be a new man. The judge had seen quiet, soft-spoken men turn in a relatively short time into loud, extroverted types, and vice versa. The effect on spouses and others with whom he lives can be imagined.

At first psychochemicals and electrotherapy were given to try to reverse the change. But this rarely seemed to work. Several unmanageable cases of schizophrenia had resulted. It was finally decided that a legal change of personality should be permitted, thus giving the patient a chance to re-establish his new personality and identity.

The next case was announced. This one, the judge felt, might not be so straightforward. A married couple had managed somehow to have an illegal child. He could already hear himself giving them a stern lecture: "You know the earth has filled up with people, and there is simply no room for children—except to replace the few unavoidable deaths that do take place each year. You are certainly well aware that that is why you, and all others on earth, have been sterilized—so that illegal births will *not* take place. Your only chance, as you well know, was through the lottery, the winners of which are legally, and temporarily, desterilized. You have not been among the winners."

And he could hear the couple's objections. "It's not our fault that those people in the twentieth century couldn't keep their population under control."

"You are quite right," he would answer. "But the fact remains that we have thirty-five billion people on this earth. We are just barely managing to feed and house everyone.

Since almost no one dies anymore, you know what would happen if even 10 per cent of the women had children. It simply cannot be allowed."

The couple was brought in—without the child. He had wanted dearly to see it—a girl, a darling baby girl, he had heard—but he knew that what he had to do would be even more difficult if he saw her. The trial went about as he expected. They had gone to an illegal desterilizer, and had had the child in hopes that they might somehow get away with it. During the trial, Judge Mann mentally queried the computer file and learned that the desterilizer had subsequently fled the country.

In spite of the seriousness of the situation, the law remained lenient in these cases. Punishment was limited to permanent sterilization for both, and removal of their names from all the lottery lists—lists for larger apartments, adopted children, and, of course, a permit to have a natural child. The child would be put up for adoption.

Judge Mann looked at his watch and decided he was taking too much time with each case. The whole point of doing away with the jury system some thirty years ago was to speed up the courts. He still had a long list of cases to get through. He wondered about the fact that although the vast majority of the population had too little to do, there were still some professions that were overloaded. He sighed, and then perked up with the thought that he wouldn't be doing this much longer anyhow. The fifty-year limit on any one career would soon be up for him.

He would once again have to go through the one-week programmed electrochemical learning course. But which one? He had already tried several sciences (each new careerist got a six-month trial period). Perhaps something in the arts? Visual poetry? His last gene-typing had shown nothing that would disqualify him in this area. Even if he chose a career that was not in keeping with his genotype, he could always take a career virus that would enter his genes and make the necessary changes. But he preferred to stay away from career viruses; they were not yet foolproof and there were sometimes undesirable side effects.

There was another problem. The usual procedure in being educated for a new career was to delearn the old one, so as to be fresh and clear for the new one. Still, there were those who maintained that we still were only using 50 per cent of our mental capacity; therefore they felt that delearning wasn't really necessary, especially in the light of computer plug-in. Andrew, unfortunately, still had one of the older types of brain socket, and delearning wasn't as easy as learning. . . .

His mind snapped back to the scene in front of him when he heard the next case announced: "The state vs. A313." A handsome woman strode into the court and stood defiantly before him.

Now, Judge Mann thought, we are going to have some action. A313 was an android, a perfectly shaped, man-made person, utterly indistinguishable from a normal human. Until now androids had been considered to be owned by those who had made them. A313 maintained that this was unfair, that children who were brought into the world eventually got their freedom. Why not androids?

In order to get the case into court, she had simply left the institution that had built her, and in which she had worked for some seven years. When she had been brought back, she simply left again. This was the first such rebellion, and of course all the other androids (there were some five hundred of them around the world) would be following the case with great interest. She had gotten the case into court by the simple expedient of claiming that she was human, and that she was being detained against her will.

Judge Mann stared, as unobtrusively as he could, at the

remarkable creature standing before him. He had never seen an android in person before. He was utterly amazed at how perfectly made she was. He found it hard to believe that she was not "human." But then, he thought, how many of us can still be called human? Most of us have had at least 50 per cent of our insides, and outsides, replaced either by artificial devices or organic transplants.

He mused: Isn't it ironic. Ten years ago, computers replaced judges in half the courts as an experiment to see whether they could handle the job. Would A313 have had a better chance if this case were being handled by one of them? I wonder if. . . .

He caught himself, popped an attention pill into his mouth, and settled down to hear the arguments.

1

Biology Yesterday, Today, and Tomorrow

BIOLOGY IS USUALLY defined as the science or the study of life. The simplicity of the definition stands in strong contrast, however, to the complexities of the subject. For one thing, there are a number of levels at which the biologist can perform his studies. The atom is the building block of all matter. In trying to understand life, the biologist might study the connection between the structure and function of an atom and the life processes. For example, all substances can be considered simply as collections of atoms that stick together by means of an electromagnetic force. Does the biologist have to deal with this concept before he can perform satisfactorily, as the radio engineer must understand electricity?

It turns out that atoms and their parts (protons, neutrons, and electrons) have traditionally been considered the province of physicists. But the biologist often uses information provided by the physicist.

At the next level, we find ourselves in the world of molecules, which are groups of atoms. Now we have invaded the traditional realm of chemists, and indeed are coming close to the level of life. For the next step up is the cell,* which is generally conceded to be the building block of life, and cells are made up of molecules. The cell is the smallest unit, or lowest level, that exhibits all the basic properties of life. It reproduces, grows, "eats," and gives off wastes.

It is at the next level up that we find tissues. These are aggregates of cells of the same kind that work together to perform a particular function. Muscle and skin tissue are good examples.

Beyond tissues we find complete organs—heart, liver, stomach. And above that we find the level that consists of complete organisms, such as dandelions, worms, birds, and people. These are studied by such specialists as herpetologists (who study snakes) and ichthyologists (who study fish).

Nor is that the end of the biologist's concern. For ants, termites, bees, and other living things, including man, sometimes group together into communities. These communities, being a part of life, affect it and so are also the concern of certain biologists, often called ecologists.

* Some biologists would insist on an intermediate step, sometimes called organelles, which includes divisions or parts of the cell that perform specialized functions. Examples are the nucleus of the cell, mitochondria, membranes, etc.

The important thing to realize is that at each of these levels there is something to be learned that affects man's total understanding of himself and the rest of the biological world.

Is Man a Machine?

During the Middle Ages it was thought that life and living things not only were beyond the comprehension of man, but would forever remain so. Thus, not only was it useless to try to fathom the workings of livings things (which is, after all, what biologists do), but it was also wrong to do so. Clearly anyone who worked in such an area was dealing with the black arts.

Still, as always, there was a brave soul here and there who was willing to go his own way. This was the case when the Englishman William Harvey came to the remarkable conclusion in 1628 that the blood circulates. Obvious? Apparently not.

The importance of this observation can hardly be overstated. It was one of the very first demonstrations that physical principles can be applied to living things. In other words, the heart was a pump, not the seat of the soul, the center of intelligence, or, as we still hear today, the symbol of love. Dr. D. E. Wooldridge, author, engineer, and businessman, suggests that "the development of science can be described as the process of transferring one after another aspect of human experience from the supernatural into the realm of natural law."

In subsequent years and centuries, we have found that each of the body's organs has some important function to perform. The stomach is involved in the digestion process, the kidneys help eliminate wastes from the body, the glands manufacture hormones and other chemical substances needed for proper operation of the body. The atoms of oxygen, carbon, and nitrogen that make up our bodies are no different from the atoms that are found in chemical fertilizers, toothbrush handles, and other inanimate objects. And the same physical and chemical laws that control the growth, decay, or activities of a non-living thing also control ours.

Is the body therefore simply a physiochemical machine? Or is there an additional, mysterious "life force" that makes a living thing different from an equivalent collection of atoms and molecules? This is the heart of a debate that has raged for centuries. The proponents of the first view, that life and life's processes are completely explainable in physical and chemical terms, are called *mechanists,* or *reductionists* (from the idea that life and life's processes are reducible to physical and chemical processes).

The opponents are called *vitalists,* from the idea that some "vital" force or principle is involved. (The Latin word for life is *vita.*)

Harvey's work, of course, struck a strong blow at the vitalist idea, as did other discoveries regarding the operation of the body.

But the vitalists could still fall back on the "obvious" difference between organic and inorganic materials. Inorganic materials were thought to be those that are clearly non-living, such as rocks and metals. Organic materials were thought of as those that comprised or were produced by living things. Examples are wood, petroleum, and urea, an animal waste product found in urine.

But then, in 1827–28, the German chemist Friedrich Wöhler created urea in the laboratory. Again vitalism went down, one would have thought permanently. But no. A living thing, even the most simple, is a fearfully complex object. A single cell—ranging typically from 0.01 to 0.05 mm. in diameter—is nothing less than a fully automated chemical processing plant. Since we have never come anywhere near being able to duplicate its incredible combination of small size and high complexity, how can we really be sure that there is *not* some secret (the "vital force") of which we are presently unaware.

Both vitalist and reductionist will agree, however, that though we have learned much, there is still much that we don't know. There is, for instance, the remarkable fact that many of the cell's components which live peacefully side by side in the cell are lethal to each other when placed together in the test tube.

There are other complications. Among the most interesting is this: You can study a rock by breaking it down into pieces and then into its smallest constituents, molecules, but it is still rock. But when you try to do the same thing to living things, you destroy the very characteristic you are supposed to be studying, namely, life.

So reductionists and vitalists continue their arguments. Is there some way out of this impasse? Suppose, just suppose, we could *create* life in the test tube. Wouldn't that prove the correctness of the reductionist's views? We shall learn in Chapter 6 of attempts to do this very thing. But we shall learn too that even here there are complications. Max Delbrück, the physicist-turned-biologist, tells us that "any one cell, embodying as it does the record of a billion years of evolution, represents more a historical than a physical event. . . . You cannot expect to explain so wise an old bird in a few simple words." In other words, we shall see that even defining what is alive and what is not presents surprising difficulties.

Beginnings of Modern Biology

A strong case can be made for the statement that modern biology really began when a German professor of anatomy, Theodor Schwann, announced in 1839 that the cell was the basis of all life, and that all the large plant and animal tissues were actually made up of cells. Indeed, the term biology only dates back to the early 1800's.

The study of the molecule became possible with the development of the electron microscope in the 1940's. But even the best electron microscope is limited, in the amount of magnification it can provide, to details in the neighborhood of one millionth of a millimeter. This is just about right for viewing some of the parts of cells, but the molecules of which the cells are composed remain indistinguishable.

Newer forms of the electron microscope, plus other techniques such as X-ray diffraction, have made it possible to actually examine molecules. This, combined with a new understanding of the principle of heredity, has spawned the field of molecular biology as we know it today.

Simplified drawing of main structures of the cell (not drawn to scale). Ribosomes are involved with production of protein, while the mitochondria, called the cell's "power plants," are where storage and release of energy takes place.

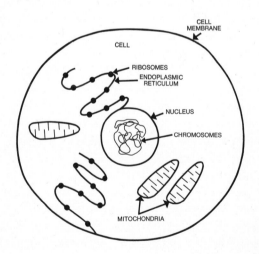

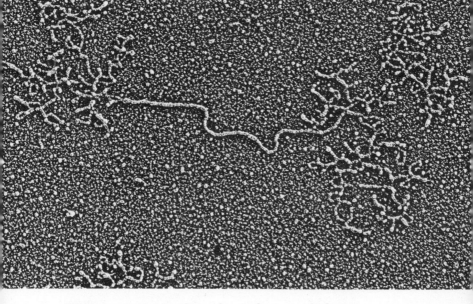

Electron microscopic photo of a single gene, which was recently isolated for the first time by a team of Harvard University scientists. The center portion is 1.4 microns long. (One micron equals one thousandth of a millimeter.)

Molecular Biology

The meaning of the term molecular biology would appear to be self-evident: the study of the life processes at the molecular level. A small problem arises, however. For it was the molecular biologists who succeeded in showing that particles of matter carry the information necessary to run living things, which has turned out to be one of the outstanding discoveries of our time, and one that is going to revolutionize our lives. This has led to a confusion of terms.

Molecular biology actually is concerned with all of life's processes, such as respiration and digestion. The term, however, is now often used to refer to the hereditary process, to the world of DNA, RNA, genes, and chromosomes, probably because of the importance and profound implications of the discovery. It is therefore also called genetics.

15

A better term would be molecular genetics. For genetics is the study of heredity, of variation and evolution, and of how and why organisms resemble and differ from their parents, other members of their species, and from all other living things. And as with biology in general, genetics can be studied at all levels. Thus in addition to molecular genetics, which deals with the way RNA and DNA control the operation and growth of living things, we have radiation genetics, population genetics, and so on.

The field of genetics could be said to have had its beginnings just about a century ago. Incredible as it may seem, scientists have been able to make remarkable guesses about molecular goings-on from observing heredity in macroscopic organisms. Thus it was with the Austrian botanist, Gregor Mendel. For his experiments were with successive generations of peas and other plants. Yet out of these large-scale experiments came his idea for the gene, which might be called the unit of heredity, and which was quite invisible at the time. Indeed, because so little was known about the subject, scientists had no matrix, or frame, into which to fit Mendel's work, and it was forgotten for some thirty years. And even at the time of its recovery, in the early 1900's, it was only the functional characteristics of heredity and genes, the statistical laws, that were known. What genes were in a physical sense was a complete mystery—and remains somewhat mysterious even today.

But even molecular biology, indeed, any scientific field, is not a single, clear-cut science. Dr. Francis Crick, one of the discoverers of just how DNA does its work, had this to say about his field: "I . . . was forced to call myself a molecular biologist because when inquiring clergymen asked me what I did, I got tired of explaining that I was a mixture of crystallographer, biophysicist, biochemist, and geneticist. . . ." *

* Stent, *The Coming of The Golden Age,* p. 36.

Implications of Molecular Biology

In any case, with the aid of this new science, man, for the first time in history, seems to be coming close to a basic understanding of such phenomena as viral infection, the workings of immunization, and aging, as well as such killers as heart disease and cancer.

The term "basic understanding" is an important one, for with it comes the ability to do things that couldn't be done before. Our ability to "build" plastics and drugs chemically is an outgrowth of our knowledge of how atoms stick together to make molecules, and how molecules stick together to make substances. Nuclear power became possible because of what we had learned about the nucleus of the atom.

The physical sciences—physics, chemistry, electronics, etc. —have, just within the last century, had a great impact on the way we live. Plastics, cars, aircraft, and television have made enormous changes in our lives. But Aldous Huxley, who wrote the remarkable science-fiction novel *Brave New World*, which foresaw many of the things we will talk about in this book, has also written, "It is only by means of the sciences of life that the quality of life can be radically changed."

And he was right. For the biologist is, sooner or later, going to rip our world to pieces. Imagine, or try to imagine, a society in which people live to age 300, or forever. Today a vice president of a company can usually see at least the possibility of becoming president in 10 or 15 years. But what if he has to wait 150 years?

And how about marriage? 170 years with the same partner?

And what will happen when parents are able to specify that they want their new child to be a boy or a girl? Most parents, especially those in the less-developed countries, want boys, who are usually stronger and better able to help with farming, chores, and so forth. Will we have a world that is 95 per cent male?

In spite of the obvious importance of these questions, it is also important to remember that modern biology is not only a matter of molecular genetics, although that aspect of biology has certainly been getting the lion's share of publicity.

Currently the problems of our environment are vying for our attention, and deservedly so.

It seems hard to believe, but biology in the future will undoubtedly be an even broader subject than it is today. Here are some examples of what may come to pass. Computers and other complex electronic devices now manufactured mechanically may well be "grown" to take advantage of nature's dexterity. The behavior of man and his societies may well be a biological consideration, rather than psychological and sociological, as at present. This is based on discoveries that show a direct connection between certain areas of the brain and particular activities, both mental and physical. For instance, rage and pleasure, as well as hunger and thirst, can now be controlled artificially. Perhaps criminals will someday be treated by biologists.

From the very small to the very large—all areas of life are fair game for biologists. From the molecules that make up our genes and our skin to the whole world that is our environment.

Within that wide span lie possibilities for increasing food production to feed an ever and rapidly increasing world population, improved handling of wastes—gas, liquid, and solid—that are rapidly fouling the world around us, improvements in the mind and body of man, and, of course, improved medical care for the sick and the aged. We start our tour of biology in the world of the future with a look at what is being done in the area of health and health care.

2

Biomedical Research

THE MAJOR OBJECTIVES of medical science are to keep the human patient alive and well. Not only are both objectives sometimes difficult to accomplish, but even defining and understanding them often presents considerable difficulty.

It seems self-evident, for instance, that we are well when we are feeling well. But this is not necessarily true. And recognition of this fact has brought a relatively new aspect of medicine, presymptomatic disease, to the fore. The idea here is that an invasion of microorganisms (or some other problem) may have begun while you are still feeling quite fit. In other words, such discomforts as fever, sore throat, aching muscles are symptoms of a disease, not the disease itself. If we could detect the invasion early, before the symptoms arise, we would have a much better chance of preventing the symptoms of the sickness from arising. Perhaps, too, a smaller dose of drugs or other remedy could be sufficient and use of many of the stronger drugs, which have unpleasant side effects, could be avoided.

To be able to do this, however, requires that we know very well what the "normal" conditions of the body are, and what the "normal" population of microorganisms is in the body. For our bodies play host to multitudes of such organisms. Fortunately most of them are quite harmless; some are even beneficial.

Although the jobs of biologist and medical researcher overlap to a large extent, we might say, roughly, that it is the task of biologists, in their attempt to understand the structures and activities of life, to define what is natural and normal in living things. The medical people are more interested in the body when things begin to go wrong. It is their job to bring it back to normal.

It seems likely that in the future there will be better ways to evaluate the "true" state of health of the body, and therefore better ways of treating deviations from that state. A recent study by the National Heart and Lung Institute, for example, showed that nearly a quarter of initial, non-fatal heart attacks went unrecognized by both the patient *and his private physician*. Some of the attacks were completely painless and therefore unnoticed, while others were confused with different ailments altogether, such as gallbladder disease or ulcer. The attacks were later diagnosed by careful, periodic examinations and electrocardiograms. The important part of the study, however, is that the unrecognized attacks were just as serious, in terms of the likelihood of future attacks and death, as were the recognized ones! Within five years of the attack, one in three of both the recognized and unrecognized types had recurred, and half of all the recurrences were fatal.

Detection and Prevention of Disease

It is tempting to predict, as others have done, that all disease will be wiped out in a hundred, or a thousand, years. We surely hope so. But this seems unlikely, at least for the foreseeable future. For one thing, it has been found that microorganisms causing certain diseases have actually changed, or adapted, to the point where a drug that was once useful against them no longer is, and new drugs have had to be developed to do the job.

There is also the problem of degenerative diseases such as high blood pressure, arthritis, stroke, and heart disease. These are not caused by infectious agents, that is, micro-organisms such as bacteria and viruses, but by normal or abnormal deterioration of the organ or body part in question. By normal, we mean deterioration caused through wear and tear, or aging. (But even here, as we shall later see, new definitions are in order.) By abnormal we mean the things people do to their bodies through the use of toxic agents such as drugs, tobacco, and alcohol. As long as this kind of thing goes on, clearly disease cannot be wiped out.

In the less-developed countries, where sanitation facilities, medical care, and drug supplies are limited, infections and contagious (catching) diseases such as cholera, typhus, and malaria are the main problems. In the Western world these have been virtually wiped out, and the degenerative diseases have become the greatest killers. Indeed, in the United States, heart disease and stroke account for something like half of deaths *from all causes* each year.

To aid the physician in his battle against such diseases, both biologists and medical researchers, as well as physicists, chemists, and engineers, have supplied and will continue to supply a vast arsenal of new equipment for detection and diagnosis. The body is after all a machine, at least in the following sense. Although a vastly complex one, it still has basic requirements of food and oxygen; and it per-forms basic functions of digestion, metabolism (the burning of food and oxygen to obtain energy and build tissue), and the elimination of wastes. Both the activities and the wastes can provide clues to the operation of the body.

This wireless monitoring system, placed at a nurse's station in a hospital, can show at a glance the state of a variety of vital functions of ten different patients. An alarm can be set to ring or light when any of these functions, such as heart rate or blood pressure, changes significantly.

The well-known stethoscope, for instance, helps the doctor listen to, among other things, the sound of the heartbeat and of the lungs as the patient breathes. From this he can tell a great number of things about the state of those vital organs.

Temperature detectors, i.e., thermometers, were another great advance in medical practice. But things haven't changed much in the almost four hundred years since they were introduced. It still takes three to five minutes to have one's temperature taken, and hospital patients are still often awakened in the middle of the night for this purpose. Nor does a thermometer identify the location or source of the illness. (A tumor, for instance, is usually warmer than the surrounding tissues.) Infrared-sensitive devices have already been constructed that will instantly identify local areas of fever or other problems, and without need to annoy the patient.

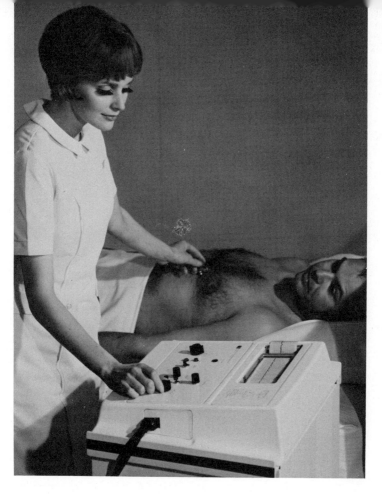

A single channel electrocardiograph.

There are a host of physical and chemical activities going on in the body—electrical, magnetic, ionic—that are being studied and may provide new leads for the medicine of the future. The electroencephalograph (EEG) and electrocardiograph (EKG) of today, which tell something of the functioning of the brain and heart from electrical waves, may well be complemented by the MEG ("magnetoencephalograph") and MKG ("magnetocardiograph") of the future, which will utilize magnetic information.

Studies of a patient's blood and urine have traditionally been used as indicators of trouble. More recently saliva has been found to be useful as well. All these fluids carry *hormones* * and can therefore provide indications of disturbances in some of the hormone-secreting glands of the body. Both the chemistry (or composition) and the flow rates of all these fluids can provide useful information. It is only by knowing the norm in all the above-mentioned cases that the information these fluids provide is at all useful.

The ultimate outcome is probably a device that evaluates all the wastes of the body, including breath, sweat, feces, and dried skin scales on a periodic basis and provides an indication of the subject's health. The evaluation is likely to be quite automatic and tied in with a central medical data bank, which will keep a medical record of each person's health for consultation in case of emergency.

Another possibility is a medical couch in the home that will provide, in addition to the chemical tests mentioned above, a quick physical check-up, heat-scope reading of temperature, heart-reading, blood pressure, and so on—all piped into a central medical computer file.

Someday it might even be possible to do all this automatically every night while you sleep. So don't be surprised if your phone rings one morning and a gentle voice suggests: "Why don't you drop in to see Dr. Jones this morning; your heart skipped a couple of beats last night."

The Heart

On the other hand, the voice might not even mention the heartbeat, for any mention of a problem with the heart is usually enough to practically frighten a person to death.

* Hormones are enormously important in the proper operation of the body. They are organic substances produced in small quantities in one part of the body that are then transported to other parts where they exert a strong effect on, and perhaps even control, a particular activity.

There are several reasons for this, not all of them medical. One is that heart disease is Western man's greatest killer. Every year well over half a million people die of heart attacks in the United States alone. But there are other, non-medical reasons as well. One is that we can "feel" our hearts beating, especially when tense, excited, or in danger.

As a result the heart has for centuries been regarded as the center of one's being. (In the eighteenth century, Antoine Rivarol wrote, "Mind is the partial side of man; the heart is everything.") In ancient civilizations, such as the Mesopotamian, the heart was considered the seat of the intellect. Others have considered it the seat of the soul, the emotions, and what have you. The fact that it is simply a pump doesn't prevent some from having similar ideas even today. You all know what the symbol of Valentine's Day is.

Thus in the late 1960's, when we began to read about heart transplants, our hearts may have jumped a bit, but in general it was felt that the medical millennium was really arriving. After all, the very definition of death was (or was generally thought to be) the cessation of heart motion.

But this criterion for death is hardly foolproof. In the brutal, dry desert of the African Kalahari where the Bushman struggles constantly for his very existence and where the knowledge of medicine is relatively shallow, it has happened more than once that a "dead" Bushman has literally risen from the shallow grave in which he was placed after his heart stopped beating.

In more advanced societies, lack of heartbeat is being used less and less often as a criterion for ascertaining death. In 1962, for instance, the great Soviet physicist Lev Landau was involved in a terrible auto accident. Four days later, in spite of all the doctors could do for him, his heart stopped beating and his blood pressure dropped to zero. But the doctors wouldn't give up. They started the heart beating again with injections and transfusions of blood. Within the following week his heart stopped beating three more times. Each time Landau was brought "back" to life. He afterwards lay in a coma for sixty days, and, until his death in 1968, bore scars from the ordeal, such as a damaged intestine from heavy doses of drugs. Yet he had been given six additional years of life, and relatively good health.

When Dr. Landau heard that the first heart-transplant patient, Louis Washkansky, had died, he commented, "What a pity. I had hoped that he would inherit from me the title of 'the most interesting patient on earth.'"

Teams of doctors today almost routinely perform what would once have been thought miracles.

How, then, can we distinguish between what is termed clinical (apparent) and biological death?

In 1968 the Council for the International Organization of Medical Science, established under the World Health Organization, laid down these criteria for death: loss of all response to the environment; complete abolition of reflexes and loss of muscle tone; cessation of spontaneous breathing; abrupt fall in the arterial blood pressure and a flat electroencephalogram (indicating no brain action). Usually a flat EEG for twenty-four hours is a sure sign of death.

But it seems that sometimes even a flat EEG is not a sufficient criterion. In Israel a 15-year-old boy received a severe brain injury as a result of a fall. By all the criteria mentioned above he should have been dead. But fortunately the doctors, by some intuition, kept the boy alive for two weeks by means of drugs and artificial respiration, in spite of the evidence presented by the EEG. One day there was a change in the EEG, the beginning of a movement back to life. He had been clinically, but not biologically, dead.

With modern medical advances it is becoming increasingly difficult to distinguish between these two states. At Hadassah Hospital in Israel it is believed that measuring the oxygen consumption of the brain may be the way to ascertain biological death. A sure method of detecting death is needed to be certain that an organ is not removed from a patient who could be resuscitated later on. Another is to prevent physicians from wasting time, effort, and money on trying to keep alive someone who is biologically dead.

Transplants

The transplantation of human hearts has probably been the most exciting medical news of the last few years. Although, at the time of this writing, only a few of the more than 130 heart-transplant patients remain alive, the significance of the accomplishment remains intact. In most cases the transplanted heart performed satisfactorily, and in some cases the patient felt better afterwards, for a while at least, than he had in years.

The Kolff total heart replacement is an experimental air-driven device.

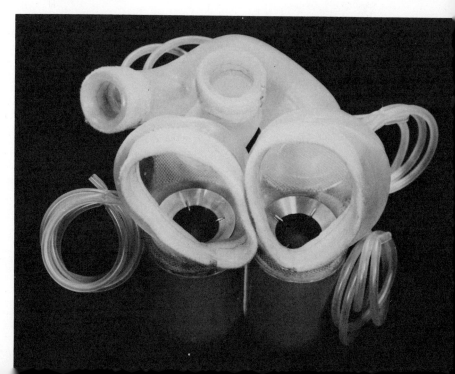

Surprisingly, the actual operation has not been the major stumbling block. The major problem has been the *rejection process*—the tendency of the body to reject foreign tissue, which someone else's heart certainly is. One way around this, and so far the most important, has been the use of *immunosuppressive* drugs—drugs that lower the tendency of the body to reject foreign tissue. Unfortunately this rejection process is part of the body's system for fighting disease. And in many transplants where "the operation was a success but the patient died," the cause was an infection, brought on by a lowered resistance. Somewhere, hopefully, there is a compromise point where the body will not reject the new organ, yet will retain enough "strength" to fight off infection. Interesting, it has been found that rejection of transplants does not take place in embryos. Perhaps something can be made of this.

Another avenue of attack has been that of trying to find a better way of matching donor and recipient. New tissue-typing tests permit a better way of doing this—in much the same way as blood is typed before transfusions. That is, the body tissues of some people "match" better than others. In the last few years we have uncovered at least six tissue types. However, except for identical twins, no perfect matches have been found. Perhaps the heart of the donor can be "preconditioned" somehow so that it won't be rejected by the recipient's rejection system.

A major problem, of course, has been that of finding suitable donors, not only for hearts, but also for kidneys, lungs, and the other organs that have been successfully transplanted. In most cases the prospective recipient is very ill, but not in immediate danger of dying. (If he were, the chances of his being able to pull through such an operation would be very unlikely.) "Plugging" the kidney patient into an external, artificial kidney machine overnight a couple of times a week can keep him going almost indefinitely. In one case, cross-circulation of a patient's blood with a baboon has kept a patient alive and cleared poisons from his blood.

It has therefore been more difficult to keep the organ intended for transplantation in good condition until it can be "put together" with the recipient than it has been to keep the recipient alive. A kidney, for instance, should be taken within ten minutes of death. But then what do you do with it?

Should the donor be an accident victim, as is often the case, it takes time before the tissue can be typed (unless this has been done earlier for some reason), a recipient (who may be quite a distance away) selected, surgery arranged, and so on. In some cases the organ can be "stored" in the dead body. A simple heart-assist device can keep blood flowing at almost normal pressure and has permitted storage of a liver for as long as four hours. Perfusion techniques (passing blood or blood substitutes through the organ's own blood vessels) are also possible. An artificial blood substitute has recently been developed and is being tried on animal organs to deliver oxygen to, and remove carbon dioxide from, the organs being preserved. Methods of freezing, of which we shall hear more later. are also being developed.* In general, the major organs cannot yet be kept in good shape for more than about a day. Certain human tissue, such as bone and cornea, can be kept for much longer periods.

To get around this problem and the rejection problem as well, other experiments have concentrated on the creation of artificial organs or the use of organs from animals. As we would expect, the rejection process is even stronger when animal organs are used, because they are more different from a human than even the most widely diversified human tissues. Nevertheless, a kidney transplanted from a chim-

---

* In some cases, people with rare blood types periodically put some of it into frozen storage to be sure there is some available for emergency use.

Small black tubes at left are man-made blood vessels which can be used as replacements for damaged arteries and veins. The material, made from a polyester velour fabric (right) coated with a bioelectric polyurethane rubber, helps prevent clotting and may find use in artificial hearts.

panzee has kept a desperately ill human alive until a suitable donor could be found.

The interaction of living tissue with artificial materials has been studied through the use of numerous, very successful metal and plastic bone and joint replacements. When passage of blood is involved, problems arise. A number of years of experience with artificial heart valves has provided much valuable information. The blood does not respond well to such treatment, and tends to adhere to the material and form clots. Information from allied, though still surprising, fields has helped to make the inserts work. It has been found, for example, that a material that was causing clots could be made to work if certain hydrodynamic principles were applied. (Hydrodynamics has to do with the motion, energy, and pressure of fluids in motion.)

One material that shows possibilities is collagen, a type of protein that constitutes more than two-fifths of the protein in our bodies. Collagen can be worked over and tailor-made into heart valves and blood vessels, and perhaps can even provide a good material for a full artificial heart. One major advantage of collagen is an unlimited supply, e.g., from animals. The material, being somewhere between animate and inanimate, might also ease the rejection process. In years to come, organs may be replaced on a regular schedule, as light bulbs are in well-maintained factories today—*before* they burn out.

Preventive Medicine

Much of what we discussed about transplants has received wide coverage in the news media. Less widely publicized are advances in diagnosis and treatment that may make such drastic steps unnecessary.

Dr. James H. Shannon, who was for several years director of the National Institutes of Health, suggested that in the future we won't need a spare-parts department in our hospitals, at least not for the majority of heart patients. Drugs that reduce blood pressure are already reducing deaths caused by certain diseases of the heart and circulatory system. There has been a startling drop of almost 50 per cent in high blood pressure deaths with the use of drugs such as guanethidine and mecamylamine.

Researchers believe they can do as well against the most common type of heart disease: the build-up of fatty deposits that clogs blood vessels (atherosclerosis), restricts the flow of blood to the heart, and finally ends in a "heart attack."

In other words, the really sensible approach would be to prevent heart disease and other illnesses rather than getting involved with all the expense, complication, and danger of a heart, kidney, or lung transplant. In 1968, Senator Walter Mondale estimated the cost of a kidney transplant at about

$5,000, as opposed to a cost of perhaps $130 per year for routine health care. And we have not even mentioned the moral issues and obvious dangers of widespread transplanting. One reporter maintains (with tongue in cheek, I trust) that patients in one hospital where heart transplants were being done became fearful of being declared dead and having their organs removed for transplantation. They put up signs when they went to sleep which stated very clearly: "I am just taking a nap."

Prevention is therefore the direction that medicine of the future must take.

Of course, there will still be accidents; and people will still mistreat their bodies; and radical treatment such as surgery will still be required, as in the cases of severed and mangled limbs. But even when they "take," re-attached limbs almost always have some impairment of function. Wouldn't it be a lot easier, neater, and better if we could *regrow* a severed or damaged finger, arm, or foot?

Impossible? Lizards and other lower animals can do it. Why can't we? The human body can already regenerate 80 per cent of its liver, as well as skin, bones, blood and hair. Why can't we simply grow a new heart? New developments in biochemistry and genetics at least point to these possibilities—and many others just as intriguing.

After all, what seems impossible today may be simple in years to come. Consider the physician of only half a century ago. He had at his command pain killers, purgatives to make patients throw up, diaphoretics to make them sweat, and tonics to build up the body, and that's all. In other words, except for a few diseases, he could treat the symptoms but not the cause! He was able to make the patient more comfortable (sometimes); and he was able to soften the effects of a disease (sometimes); but rarely was he able to cure it. The body had to do that on its own. Sometimes it did— and sometimes it didn't.

At that time infectious diseases such as tuberculosis were the major killers. In 1917 there were over eight thousand cases of pulmonary tuberculosis in Massachusetts, of which more than half died. In 1966, thanks to antibiotics, there were nine cases, of which none died.

The discovery of antibiotics constitutes one of the great advances in medicine. The ability to manufacture antibiotics on a large scale (currently a biological program in which they are grown in living tissue) is a marvel all its own. But we are improving them artificially, and even synthesizing them (creating them artificially from inorganic matter), a great advance in biochemistry.

Linus Pauling, Nobel Prize winner in chemistry, has suggested that this can be carried even further. In general, infectious diseases are caused by antigens in our blood. These are protein molecules produced or carried by toxic micro-organisms. After we have succeeded in determining the structure of such a protein molecule, Dr. Pauling says, we will then be able to make a straightforward attack upon specific diseases. (Presently, drugs are tried out on diseases on a strictly hit-and-miss basis.) We could then plot the molecular structure of a desired drug in such a way that it would interact specifically with the abnormal protein molecule that is causing the disease. This could eliminate many of the undesirable side effects now caused by many drugs.

We have not yet mentioned four other aspects of biomedicine: hereditary defects, aging, cancer, and viral diseases. As recently as a decade or two ago, there would have been no reason to consider them as a group. Today, as a result of new researches into genetics, they are recognized as closely related phenomena.

Before we can discuss them more fully, therefore, we must delve a bit more deeply into what has been happening in genetics.

33

3

Molecular Genetics

COMPUTER TERMINOLOGY RECOGNIZES two major classes of equipment. One consists of the *hardware*—the physical devices such as cabinets, wiring, memory devices. This is what most people have in mind when they think of computers. The other class, which computer men know to be just as important (and just as expensive) as the hardware, is the *softwear*. This class is made up of the systems, programs, and instructions that make the computers run and tell them what to do.

The same holds with living things. There is the physical equipment of the body, which includes the bones, muscles, tendons. This is the hardware.

But we have pointed out that each and every cell is a chemical factory. A factory needs instructions if it is to operate on schedule and not burn itself out, or operate at all. It must turn on and off; sometimes it must operate at reduced levels, as when we sleep, or at increased levels, as when we are running or in danger.

Further, most cells in the body must divide and reproduce themselves at intervals. They have to know when to do this.

Clearly we are speaking of a complex set of instructions. And so far we have spoken only of single cells. But we are multicellular creatures. Our cells must fit together into a predetermined pattern if we are to be humans and not apes or fish, or even an undifferentiated mass of cells (a tumor). Our cells must work together and under control if we are to grow, work, or rest. This means that somehow they must cooperate with each other, even though they may be performing their usual chores of turning food and oxygen into energy, or building protein for a growing boy or girl, or simply reproducing themselves to make up for cells that are constantly dying.

Construction and Operation of the Body

When I was young I learned that the three major components of the body were starches, fats, and proteins. Starches, along with sugars, provide the immediate energy needs of the body. (Both starches and sugars fall into a class called *carbohydrates*, meaning a compound of carbon and water.) Fats, sometimes called *lipids*, provide lubrication where needed (as in the joints), insulation against cold, and energy storage capability; the body stores energy in the form of lipids, which are broken down when necessary.

The word *protein* means "of first importance." Although it was always clear that the body couldn't get along without any of the components already mentioned, proteins, because they make up the structural material of the body, were considered to be the most important constituent. There is also an important class of proteins in our bodies called catalysts or, more specifically, enzymes, which are absolutely essential to the proper functioning of the body.

In chemistry, a catalyst is defined as a substance that alters the rate at which a chemical reaction would normally occur, but that remains itself unchanged by the reaction.

Some Commercial Enzymes and Their Uses

Enzyme	Source	Industry and Application
Amylase	Animal (pancreas)	Pharmaceutical: digestive aids
		Textile: desizing agent
	Plant (barley malt)	Baking: flour supplement
		Brewing: distilling, and industrial alcohol: mashing
		Food: precooked baby foods
		Pharmaceutical: digestive aids
		Textile: desizing agent
	Fungi (Aspergillus niger, A. Orzyae)	Baking: flour supplement
		Brewing: distilling, and industrial alcohol: mashing
		Food: precooked baby foods, syrup manufacture
		Pharmaceutical: digestive aids
	Bacteria (Bacillus subtilis)	Paper: starch coatings
		Starch: cold-swelling laundry starch
		Laundry: stain removal
Bromelain	Plant (pineapple)	Food: meat tenderizer
		Pharmaceutical: debriding agent
Cellulase and hemicellulase	Fungi (asperigillus niger)	Food: preparation of liquid coffee concentrates
Dextransucrase	Bacteria (Leuconostoe mesenteroides)	Pharmaceutical: preparation of blood plasma extenders, and dextran for other uses.
Ficin	Plant (fig latex)	Pharmaceutical: debriding agent
Glucose oxidase (Plus catalase or peroxidase)	Fungi (Aspergillus niger)	Pharmaceutical: test paper for diabetes
		Food: glucose removal from egg solids

Enzyme	Source	Industry and Application
Invertase	Yeast (Saccharomyces cerevisiae)	Candy: prevents granulation of sugars in soft-center candies
		Food: artificial honey
Lactase	Yeast (Saccharomyces fragilis)	Dairy: prevents crystallization of lactose in ice cream and concentrated milk
Lipase	Fungi (Aspergillus niger)	Dairy: flavor production in cheese
Papain	Plant (papaya)	Brewing: stabilizes chill-proof beer
		Food: meat tenderizer
Pectinase	Fungi (Aspergillus niger	Wine and fruit juice: clarification
Penicillinase	Bacteria (Bacillus cereus)	Medicine: treatment of allergic reactions to penicillin; diagnostic agent
Pepsin	Animal (hog stomach)	Food: animal feed supplement
Protease	Animal (pancreas)	Dairy: prevents oxidized flavor
		Food: protein hydrolysates
		Leather: bating
		Pharmaceutical: digestive aids
		Textile: desizing
	Animal (pepsin)	Brewing: beer stabilizer
	Animal (resin)	Dairy: cheese
	Animal (trypsin)	Pharmaceutical: wound debridement
	Fungi (Aspergillus oryzae)	Baking: bread
		Food: meat tenderizer
	Bacteria (Bacillus subtilis)	Baking: modification of cracker dough
		Brewing: clarifier
		Laundry: stain remover
Streptodornase	Bacteria (Streptocuccus pyogenes)	Pharmaceutical: wound debridement

For obvious reasons a catalyst is almost always used to speed up a reaction. In the chemical industry finely divided metals and oxides of metals are widely used. Often, use of a catalyst permits chemical reactions to take place that would otherwise require a high (and inconvenient) temperature to make them "go." Basically, the catalyst provides a "stage," a convenient place, for the reaction to take place.

It should therefore be easy to see that the body would have great use for catalysts. For one thing, an enormous number of chemical reactions are constantly taking place in the body. For another, the temperature of the human body is very low (in chemical terms). Without enzymes our bodies couldn't possibly carry out the multitude of jobs they do in a time that would permit ordinary living to take place.

In truth, we do not yet really know how enzymes do their jobs. They have to have a highly wrinkled structure that is shaped in a specific way to fit the molecular structure of the substances they work on. Some enzymes can join or break up thousands of molecules per second, far faster than any known industrial catalyst. Indeed, chemists trying to do the same things would have to use high temperatures, corrosive acids, and extended times to accomplish what a tiny enzyme molecule can accomplish in a fraction of a second. Enzymes in our digestive system break up food particles so efficiently that less acid is required than would otherwise be necessary, thus protecting the intestinal linings from damage. Other enzymes put some of these particles back together into other forms and combinations to replace old cells or build new ones.

Remarkable. There are probably millions of different enzymes; and a single cell might contain thousands of each of a thousand different enzymes. Who, or what, decides which enzymes will be where? Enzymes eventually "wear out." Who, or what, decides when to build new ones? And which ones to build? How, in other words, does our body know when to do what?

Naturally, the same questions may be asked about the entire operation of the body, including everything from the healing of a cut to growth to heredity.

Of First Importance

It turns out that giving the accolade "of first importance" to proteins was a little premature. It had been thought for a time that proteins somehow provided directions for operation of the body by themselves. But this has turned out not to be true. Another material, the only other structural material in our bodies aside from protein, has taken over as the "top cat" in biology.

This material is *nucleic acid,* so named because of its acidic properties and the fact that many of its most interesting properties occur in the nuclei of cells. Although nucleic acid was discovered just over one hundred years ago, it was only relatively recently that its real importance as the substance of which the gene is composed was revealed. It has been found that nucleic acid comes in two basic forms. In 1953 the scientific team of James D. Watson and Francis H. C. Crick figured out the shape of one of its subforms, *deoxyribonucleic acid* (DNA), and molecular biology exploded into the important science it is today. For the proper functioning of every cell in the body, and the body as a whole, is controlled by DNA.

DNA can be compared to the tape in a tape recorder or computer. That is to say, it contains all the instructions necessary for the proper functioning of the device. In living things this refers to the functioning of the cell at any one moment, and it refers to its activities over time, such as growth and division for reproduction.

The tape analogy is a useful one because it also covers another, and very important, characteristic of DNA, which is that it can provide a duplicate of itself. In biology form and function often go hand in hand. Thus when Watson and Crick figured out the structure of DNA, they also saw immediately how it is able to provide an ordered functioning of the body, not only throughout the life span of the individual, but from generation to generation. The secret of heredity, of how living things pass their characteristics on to their offspring, had finally been discovered.

The Double Helix

A molecule of nucleic acid is very much like a string of beads. As shown, each bead, called a *nucleotide,* consists of three smaller molecules: a sugar, a phosphate, and a third molecule called a base. The first two simply alternate along the string and form the structural backbone of the string. It is in the base, or rather sequence of bases, that the information is carried and that the great trick of reproduction is carried out.

Watson and Crick found that a molecule of DNA was actually a double row of nucleotides formed in the shape of a twisted ladder. The alternating sugar/phosphate molecules make up the sides of the ladder, and the bases constitute the

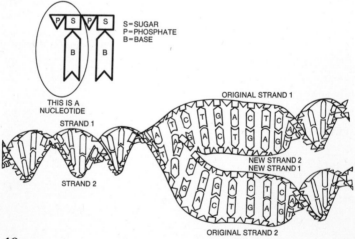

rungs. As you can see in the left side of the diagram, a base on one side of the ladder is bonded or attached to a corresponding base on the other. Since a single spiraling line is called a helix, the twisted ladder shown here has come to be called the *double helix.*

Of particular interest is the fact that there are only four different types of bases. The information that determines both the structure and operation of the entire body therefore depends upon the sequence of only four different bases along one side of the DNA molecule.

This sequence constitutes a message, just as a series of dots and dashes in the Morse code constitutes a message. And just as a series of dots and dashes can spell out any story you like, so too can the sequence of bases spell out the "story" of a human being, an ant, or a blade of grass. But it is rather a long story; human DNA contains on the order of three billion nucleotides.

The four bases in DNA are called adenine, guanine, cytosine, and tyrosine (A, G, C, and T for short).

If the sequence along one side of the ladder can tell the entire story, what is the use of the second side? This was the secret of Watson's and Crick's discovery. Each of the bases can only bond to one other kind. A to T, G to C, C to G, and T to A. Clearly, then, all the information along one side is simply repeated on the other side, but in reverse!

Can you think of any other case where information in reverse may be of value? A printing press is one. A more apt illustration for our purposes, however, is that of a mold. Suppose an artist makes a beautiful piece of statuary and wants to make several exact copies of it to give out as Christmas presents. What does he do? Does he try to sculpt five new duplicates one after the other? No. He makes a mold of the original, one that contains all the information in the original, but in reverse. Then he can make as many duplicates, or casts, as he wants to.

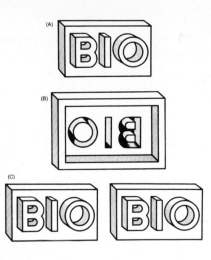

Principle of artist's mold: a) originals; b) mold contains all information (shape, size, etc.); c) castings are exact copies of originals.

This is the basic idea of the double helix. For when it comes time for the cell to reproduce itself, the DNA strands begin to unwind at one end and to split down the middle, as a zipper is unzipped. Each side is then able to pick out of the surrounding medium nucleotides of the proper type (where they have thoughtfully been placed by the system) and to build up two new chains as shown. Thus we have two DNA molecules where only one existed before.

On a larger scale, this is how cells reproduce themselves. For chromosomes, which are seen in every illustration of cells in the process of reproduction, have been seen to be primarily long strands of DNA, while genes are simply coded sequences of a thousand or so nucleotides strung out along the way.

It is from the word gene, of course, that the term genetics has come, for the traits of an organism (color, size, number of legs, arms, fingers) are controlled by these specific sequences of nucleotides along the strand. Roughly speaking, each trait is controlled by a group of nucleotides, i.e., a gene.

42

Further, there is not one long string of genes. Rather, the genes are contained in a number of separate "packages," the chromosomes. Thus certain genes (and hence traits) are linked and are inherited as a group, while others (in other chromosomes) are not. The cell of each kind of organism contains a specific number of chromosomes. In humans, the number is 46 (23 pairs), while frogs have 26, and corns cells have 20.

One Gene, One Enzyme

With the single exception of the female egg cell, not a single one of the billion or so cells in a human body is large enough to be seen with the naked eye. Yet within the even smaller nucleus of each cell there lies the DNA that contains all the instructions necessary for the bodily operations, including growth and reproduction. This tangled "thread of life," although only a few molecules wide, would be three or four feet long if straightened out!

The scene shifts now outside the nucleus, and we zero in on a protein molecule somewhere in the rest of the cell. We find something very interesting. The protein, no matter which one of the thousands of different kinds we happen to be looking at, turns out to be a string of smaller molecules called *amino acids*. As with the nucleotides along DNA, the amino acids are arranged, bead-like, end to end along a linear chain and then rolled up into a ball.

Decoding the "instructions" for a protein.

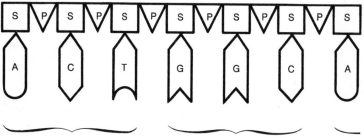

1ST CODE WORD   2ND CODE WORD

The similarity between the two chains, DNA and amino acid,* suggests a method for transcribing the information contained inside the nucleus to the final product, an enzyme or a protein, in the cell. The nucleotides, i.e., the bases, it turns out, are "read" in sequence (rung after rung) in groups of three. Each group of three stands for a single amino acid. In this way the DNA molecule spells out the proper sequence of amino acids.

As shown, the base sequence ACTGGCATC can be decoded as a "sentence" containing three "words": ACT, GGC, and ATC. ACT is the code for one particular amino acid, GGC is the code for another, and so on. There are about twenty different amino acids, from which the thousands of different proteins are constructed. The average protein contains perhaps three hundred amino acids. From the point of view of the DNA, however, we would say that the average "sentence" contains about three hundred "words."

Although we do not know all the details of how the message is carried, the major characteristics have been figured out. Indeed, bridging the gap between the sequence of "letters" in the genetic material and the final amino acid chain has probably been the outstanding discovery of the last decade. Broadly, what happens is this. In a manner similar to the splitting of DNA prior to reproduction, DNA produces the second major form of nucleic acid, which is called *ribonucleic acid* (RNA). It is RNA that carries the message from the genes inside the nucleus (the "executive office") to the factory outside, telling the various divisions what to do and when.*

To see how RNA does this, we return to the analogy of the artist's mold. RNA, performing the function of the mold, carries the message in reverse. RNA then breaks away from

---

* The technical term for the chain of amino acids is polypeptide.
* A recent report in the British journal *Nature* suggests there are some cases, such as in cancer, in which RNA directs the production of DNA. But in general DNA is still the "master chemical."

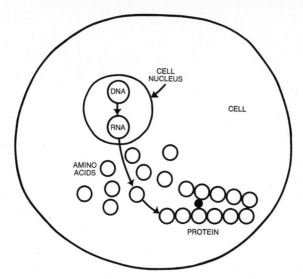

How DNA directs synthesis of proteins.

DNA, physically travels outside the nucleus, and acts as a template or mold for the actual construction of an amino acid chain. Thus the original genetic directions indirectly act to cause the addition of one amino acid at a time to the string of amino acids being built in the cell. The result is one of the thousands of different kinds of proteins needed to keep the body in shape and in operation.

The DNA chains may also tell us something about the behavioral patterns of living things. It has been found that at least some birds brought up in soundproof rooms will sing in a way that is basically correct and specific to their species. Is it possible that the notes are represented, one by one, along the DNA chain in one of their chromosomes?

In the case of protein, however, it is not only the sequence of the amino acids, but also the shape of the final product that is important. It is the combination of sequence and shape that determines whether the protein will be hair, nail, muscle, hemoglobin, or what have you.

What is especially noteworthy is that every cell in the body is believed to contain all the genetic instructions for the whole

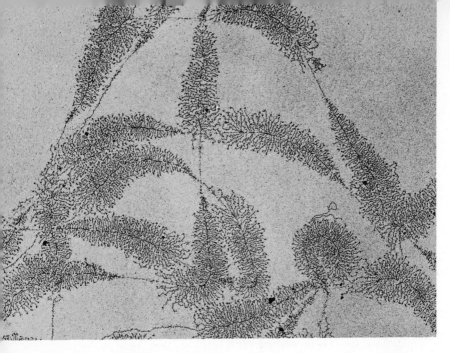

Electron microscope photograph of genes from a South African Clawed Toad, show about 25,000 times actual size. The genes are the spines of the carrot-shaped objects which are linked together like beads along a necklace. The photo shows genes in the process of producing molecules of RNA. Each gene is producing about 100 molecules of RNA (the hair-like fibers extending from the genes). These will eventually find their way outside the cell and be used in the formation of protein.

body! But of course not all of the instructions are in force all the time. For example, a certain hormone may be necessary for body growth or development of a beard. The hormone is simply not manufactured until the proper moment comes when some action or other triggers the proper cells to make it.

If we should succeed in completely understanding the genetic code, it is conceivable that we could figure out from a single cell all the inherited characteristics of a person: color of hair and eyes, the shape of the head and face, even the potential intelligence. Knowing this, we might be able to make changes! We will talk of some possible methods later.

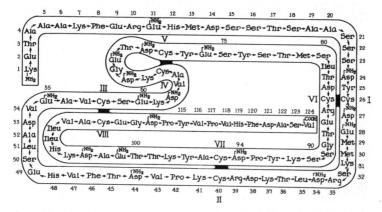

Chemical structure of bovine (cow) ribonuclease, an enzyme secreted by the pancreas for digesting RNA. As shown by the numbers, this enzyme consists of 124 amino acids. To save space in the drawing they have been abbreviated to three letters (Lys=lysine, etc.). In the enzyme the amino acids are not only placed end to end in a polypeptide chain, but also are folded into a three dimensional structure and crosslinked at four places, as indicated by the blackened areas. This represents the first time that an enzyme has been synthesized in a laboratory. The work was done by teams of workers at Rockefeller University and Merck and Company.

Since all the information for an organism is contained in a single cell, then something else of interest could be done, and that is to re-create an entire organism from one or more such cells. Everyone who works in a garden, for example, knows that it is possible to take a cutting from a plant and grow a whole new plant from it. The Greek word for a cutting or twig is *clone,* and this word has been applied to the as yet imaginary human duplicate of a living being. (Obviously the clone, derived from a single "parent," will be exactly like her —or him!)

Modern work along these lines was started by Professor F. C. Steward of Cornell University. Working with individual carrot cells, he was able to grow complete new carrots, with roots, green shoots, and all.

In another experiment, Dr. J. B. Gurdon of Oxford University took an unfertilized egg cell from a frog and destroyed its nucleus with ultraviolet light. The egg cell, remember, would have only half the proper number of chromosomes. Then Dr. Gurdon took a body cell, e.g., an intestinal cell, from *another frog*, removed its nucleus by means of some highly delicate surgery performed while looking through a microscope, and implanted the nucleus into the original, enucleated egg cell. The egg cell suddenly "saw" a full complement of chromosomes and was apparently tricked into thinking it had been fertilized. It then went on to produce a fine baby tadpole—which grew up to be a perfect duplicate of, not the

Dr. Robert Bruce Merrifield, Professor of the Rockefeller University, adjusting the control panel of the automated peptide synthesizer. This device is used in synthesizing ribonuclease.

frog that laid the egg, but the one that contributed the intestinal cell.

Human cloning presents considerably more difficulty than that of carrots and frogs, for several reasons. One is that human egg cells must be carried in the womb, whereas frog eggs are adapted for external existence. Moreover, human cells are more specialized than those of carrots and frogs. The more specialized a cell, such as a skin cell, has become, the less likely that it can be used as the "parent" for a complete organism.

Still, it would be foolish to say that human cloning will not be accomplished. The question of *why* and *whether* it should be done is another problem altogether. A dictator may want to build an army of fighters, or a baseball manager a team of Babe Ruths. Clearly, this raises social issues. Even were there no social issues, however, the possibility of producing Einsteins or Churchills is doubtful, for the individual is not a product only of his heredity. He is also a product of his environment. Professor Salvador Luria of M.I.T. tells us that "the function of the genes in a cell is regulated by the [internal] environment, including the action of other genes in the same cell, the chemical messages from other cells, and also the external environment such as food and temperature."

The late Dr. Jean Rostand of the French Academy once suggested that everyone set aside a few body cells to serve as the ultimate sort of life insurance. But to what purpose? A widow, for example, would not then have her husband back. She would simply have another child.

On the other hand, she could be absolutely certain of what she was getting in a physical sense, including the sex of the child. Secondly, there may be good medical reasons for wanting to produce a child without including the genetic material from one of the parents. We shall see in the next chapter how this capability would be useful.

There is one other idea that we should mention before we leave the subject of cloning. To get around the transplant-rejection problem, we might consider the possibility of cloning of organs. If we could somehow get a cell from each of our organs, we could grow duplicates of them in case of emergency. Equivalently, a complete clone would provide a source of spare parts.

Troubles

The magic of the DNA system is that something as complicated as a cell can reproduce itself exactly, manufacture the proper substances in the proper quantities and at the right times, and so on. But if some of the information contained in DNA becomes mixed up or lost, all the functions that come later—the formation of RNA, and then protein synthesis—would go wrong. The cell may then function incorrectly or die, which could trigger a chain reaction that affects the entire body.

One possibility is that the damage will affect the mechanism that controls reproduction of the cell; if the cell begins to divide uncontrollably we may have the beginnings of either a benign or malignant tumor. Or the cell might begin to manufacture substances that are harmful to the body. This could lead to a variety of problems such as heart disease. And, as we shall see later, problems with DNA lie at the heart of at least one explanation for aging.

Finally, if the cell which is affected happens to be a germ cell—one that, when fertilized, will become a child—then the child may be affected in one or more ways. Let us look at some of these possibilities, and what may one day be done about them.

4

Genetic Disorders

IT WAS ONCE thought that a human being started life as a miniature person and simply grew larger and larger. In other words, it was thought that the original egg (or sperm) cell contained all the parts, but in miniature.

Today we know that this is not so. The original egg cell is just that, a cell. Although it is the largest cell in the human body, and is just visible to the unaided human eye, there is no way to detect a head, a foot, or a finger.

But after fertilization by a human sperm, the most remarkable phenomenon in all of nature begins its stately process. The cell divides once, and becomes two cells. The two cells divide and become four. Again and again the cells divide. At a certain point, they not only divide but begin to *differentiate* —to become specialized cells which in turn lead to the formation of muscle and other kinds of tissue.

At the end of just thirty-three divisions, a complete human being is shaped, with two five-fingered hands, two eyes, and even hair.

In other words, from the original egg cell, with instructions from the sperm cell, a complete, functioning normal human child arises—most of the time.

Unfortunately, out of approximately 4 million infants born in the United States each year, at least one in sixteen, or 250,000, are born with important birth defects. These include such problems as deafness, blindness, heart trouble, and nervous and muscular disorders. Sometimes, to complicate the matter, the symptoms do not arise until later on in life.

And of these quarter of a million children, about one in five can blame their defects on heredity; that is, their problems arise because of some defect in their genes which they inherited from their parents. The other defects arise from environmental causes—infectious disease, drugs, radiation, chemical poisons. It is estimated that 15 million persons in the United States have one or more birth defects that affect their daily lives.

Thanks to modern medical and sanitation techniques, infectious diseases have become less and less important as causes of death in children, and genetic diseases have consequently risen in importance. Today one childhood death in five is caused by some genetic disorder. Almost worse is the heartbreak and stress caused to the rest of the family by the birth and raising of children with non-fatal, though serious, problems.

Until quite recently, physicians could usually do little more than sympathize with these children and their parents. In some cases it was possible to tell a *prospective* mother and father that on the basis of their family histories, the odds were 50-50 that they would have a defective child, or 25 per cent, or whatever. These were statistical odds, based on previous experience and knowledge of statistical genetics—the same field in which Mendel originally did his work on peas.

Today genetics is a much more advanced science. Biologists and medical researchers have successively "opened up" the cell, the cell nucleus, the chromosome, and the gene. They have even begun to understand the working of genes.

Control of Genetic Disease

As often occurs in the physical sciences, with understanding comes the possibility of control. It had long been known, for instance, that there were various types of mental retardation. No one had been able to pinpoint a cause for *any* type of mental illness. Recently, however, the cause of one form of juvenile mental illness was found. Interestingly, the cause turns out to have nothing to do with the brain.

The disease was first recognized as a distinct illness about thirty-five years ago by a Norwegian scientist who noticed a strange odor coming from children who had it. Later it was found they lacked a gene that produces a liver enzyme which normally aids in the conversion of the amino acid, phenylalanine, into another, tyrosine. If either parent has only one such gene, he or she is a carrier * but is not afflicted, since the other gene in the pair (one from the mother, one from the father) can produce enough of the enzyme to keep him or her in good health. If two such carriers marry, however, the offspring have a one in four chance of having the disease, which is called phenylketonuria, or PKU. The result is an accumulation of phenylalanine which leads to poisoning of the brain and body, leading to retardation and eventual death. It was the excess of the chemical in the urine of the child that led to the peculiar odor.

But PKU can now be detected at birth with a simple test. If it is seen to be present, the child is placed on a diet low in phenylalanine and can usually lead a relatively normal life.

Although not all those afflicted respond well to the treatment, it has worked well enough that many states now require that all newborn infants be tested for this condition. It is also

---

* A carrier is one who can pass on the defective gene or genes, but who is not himself affected.

likely that testing for an increasing number of genetic diseases will become routine in coming years.

What is important here is that this type of testing holds not only for the one who is already affected but for the carriers (parents) and the unborn children as well. That is, they can all be tested and any necessary action taken.

Clearly it is of the utmost importance to two prospective parents to know the probability of their child's being born with a very serious genetic disease. Since there are ways of avoiding genetic tragedy, for example, adoption and artificial insemination, it might be best for some couples to consider not having natural children.

Until recently it was normally not possible, however, for a couple to know for sure whether they were carriers of a hereditary defect. But progress has been so rapid that each year a number of new tests become available for use in genetic diagnosis and counseling.

Let us look at a true case, reported in *The New York Times,* and see how this might work. A lady, whom we shall call Mrs. Jones, recently visited the office of Dr. Henry L. Nadler and asked, "If I have children, will they be mentally retarded?" She explained that of four children in her family she was the only one who was normal. Her three sisters were all affected by a genetic disease called Down's syndrome or, more commonly, mongolism.

She came to Dr. Nadler because he is a member of a rapidly increasing fraternity of genetic counselors. Such counselors may be physicians who have become interested in the field, or they may be biomedical researchers. In either case, their objective is to give advice to married people who have problems like Mrs. Jones's.

Dr. Nadler pointed out that even with the tremendous advances that have been made in recent years, he still could not give her a certain answer. Much depended on her family history, on her husband's family history, and on chance!

He took a detailed family history. Who else in her family was affected by Down's syndrome? In her husband's family? (This information is not as easy to obtain as it may seem. People tend to forget or ignore or hide it.) Then he made a detailed examination of Mrs. Jones's chromosomes.

The analysis showed a 30 per cent probability that the child would be afflicted with the disease.

Fortunately, although the child in the womb was once as inaccessible as the center of the earth, this is no longer so, and there are ways to test the fetus to see if it is afflicted with genetic disease. If so, the child can be aborted and the mother can try again.

Under the circumstances, Mrs. Jones decided to take a chance. After she became pregnant, she returned to the doctor's office, and underwent a process called *amniocentesis*. The technifue consists of obtaining, with a needle, a sample of the amniotic fluid in which the developing baby is floating. Analysis of the fluid, which contains cells given off in various ways by the fetus, showed that the child would be a boy— and that he would have the syndrome.

A therapeutic abortion (one given for medical reasons) was decided upon and carried out. Some months later she became pregnant again and the process was repeated. This time the child was a girl who most likely would be normal. The story ends happily with the birth of a normal, healthy girl.

The technique of amniocentesis is being applied more and more. Today perhaps two dozen genetic disorders can be diagnosed in this way. If a treatment is known, it can be carried out. If not, and the genetic problem is a serious one, then a therapeutic abortion can be performed. However, it must be pointed out that abortion is a sore subject in most of the United States, and at the time of this writing such abortions are still only permitted in a small number of states. Until very recently the physician could only depend on Mendelian genetics and give a probability of incidence. Legislators

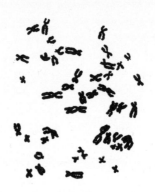

1	2	3		4	5	X

6	7	8	9	10	11	12

13	14	15	16	17	18

19	20	21	22	Y

When chromosomes of a baby girl (top) are arranged
in order, the result is called a karyotype.

didn't like the idea of aborting children on probabilities. But as prenatal testing becomes better known and more reliable, it is likely that this will change.

It is even possible that certain diseases could be completely eliminated in this manner. Dr. Kurt Hirschhorn, president of the American Society of Human Genetics, took a look at two of the most common inherited diseases in this country, cystic fibrosis and sickle cell anemia. He cites calculations which show that if all unborn children afflicted by or carrying the genes for these diseases could be identified and aborted over the next forty years, these genes could be eliminated completely and the diseases wiped out.

Amniocentesis and other genetic tests may also provide alternatives to abortion in certain cases. If two people who are carriers of the same disease-producing gene mate, the chance that a child they produce will have the disease is one in four. Some diseases are sex-linked. A form of muscular dystrophy (degeneration of the muscles) and hemophilia (insufficient blood-clotting due to lack of a substance called antihemophilic globulin) almost always occur in boys. If a woman is a carrier and her child is a boy, he stands a 50 per cent chance of being born with the disease.

Sex Determination

In such cases it would be desirable to be able to detect the sex of the child early in the pregnancy. (Amniocentesis only works after several months.) Even better would be a way of controlling the sex of the unborn child—to decide on the desired sex and then be able to produce it.

One possibility, already mentioned, is cloning. But then the results are limited to duplication of the father, unless you are willing to produce another carrier, as a clone of the mother would certainly be. Further, the marvelous possibilities inherent in the blending of two people's genes are also lost.

Scientists at Cambridge University recently performed an interesting experiment with rabbits. They removed embryos a few days old from pregnant rabbits and snipped off a few cells. Careful examination under a microscope revealed whether the embryos were male or female. The experimenters then re-implanted the embryos of the desired sex (male or female), and several were later born normally.

While this technique is obviously impractical for humans, it does seem to be a step along the way toward sex determination.

Since the sex of an offspring is determined by the chromosomes in the male sperm, the logical place to begin the search for sex determination is with the male sperm. The problem is that the male cell is much smaller and harder to work with than the egg. Nevertheless, some differences have been found between "male" and "female" sperm. Perhaps some kind of "filter" can be built that will permit only the desired type of sperm to fertilize the egg. Or the two types of sperm might be separated by some laboratory device and then the egg fertilized by artificial insemination. Or—why not?—the fertilization might be made to take place in a test tube where greater control is possible, and the egg then implanted directly into the womb. And, finally, the nightmare depicted so vividly by Aldous Huxley in his *Brave New World*—test-tube babies. Here the mother is dispensed with altogether and the embryos are brought to term (one could hardly call it birth) in a completely artificial container. In the novel this was done to make it simpler to manipulate the embryos, making a few chosen ones superior and most—those destined to be workers —inferior.

But, as in all developments, there are positive as well as negative applications. How about the woman who cannot, for

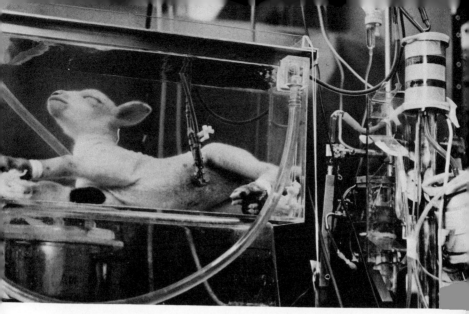

A lamb, removed from its mother's womb, is shown submerged and not breathing, but resting comfortably in a tank of synthetic amniotic fluid in the National Heart and Lung Institute's Laboratory of Technical Development. The lamb is being provided total respiratory support by an "artificial placenta" system developed in this laboratory. The system, which features a new type of artificial lung (or blood oxygenator—the pint-sized cylindrical objects on the right), has provided such total support for periods in excess of 2 days (up to 55 hours) in previous experiments.

medical reasons, go through a complete pregnancy? Is she to be denied having a child of her own? Professor Etienne Wolff, Director of the Laboratory of Experimental Biology in France, goes even further. He says:

artificial incubation . . . could make it possible to save fetuses that would otherwise die, to stimulate the intellectual and physical qualities of a child before its birth, to repair congenital [inborn] malformations, to immunize infants against infection by premature vaccination, and even to develop tolerance to foreign tissue so that they will be able to accept grafts in later life.

59

Professor H. Bentley Glass, of The State University of New York, adds:

> Only by studying the development of the human embryo and fetus under continuous observation and under various conditions can medical scientists really learn what factors produce particular kinds of abnormalities and how these may be corrected or avoided.

In any case, it is likely that sex determination will in the future be possible on a routine basis. But this will undoubtedly result in an extremely lopsided balance of male and female numbers; most people, especially in farming and less developed areas, want boys.

I leave that for you to ponder, for we have more immediate problems at hand. At the moment, even tests for genetic defects are still far too complicated and costly for routine screening. The PKU situation, for example, was originally thought to be a simple matter that had been taken care of. This has turned out not to be the case; a number of biochemical complications have cropped up. There is also some evidence that the special diet produces problems of its own. And Professor L. L. Heston of the University of Iowa Medical School points out in *Science* magazine that the "most completely known genetic disease in humans, glucose-6-phosphate dehydrogenase deficiency, occurs in at least 18 variants, each one presumably due to an amino acid substitution at a different place in the same enzyme."

As a result, for a while at least, screening will only be employed if there is some reason to suspect that an offspring might be born with a genetic defect.

On the other hand, as we mentioned earlier, most birth defects are not transmitted genetically; that is, they are not due to heredity. Often an obvious environmental cause can be found. An all-too-common, and often bitter, example, is that of rubella, or German measles. Although it is not in itself a dangerous disease, if a woman contracts rubella during the first third of her pregnancy there is a strong chance that her child will be deaf, have cataracts on the eyes, or be born with some other major problem. In 1964 a rubella epidemic in the United States caused some 50,000 abnormal pregnancies, malformations, and stillbirths. Fortunately, an anti-rubella vaccine has been developed that will cut down on this dreaded problem.

Viral DNA

Interestingly, rubella is caused by a virus. But the active agent in a virus is nucleic acid! Indeed, viruses turn out to be DNA or RNA wrapped in a coat of protein. They operate by attaching themselves to the membrane of a cell and injecting the nucleic acid into the cell. The effect is that of a change of executive leadership in a factory, or a change of a tape in a computer. The instructions contained within the viral nucleic acid take over management of the cell, which then begins to manufacture more viruses instead of the materials needed to sustain the cell. Within a half hour, up to several hundred new viruses have been made. These then burst out of the cell and can now infect other cells. Some forms of cancer, such as leukemia, have been shown to be produced by viruses.

Clothed in anti-contamination garb and wearing goggles as protection against germ-killing ultraviolet rays, technicians pool virus harvests during the production of vaccine against German measles (rubella).

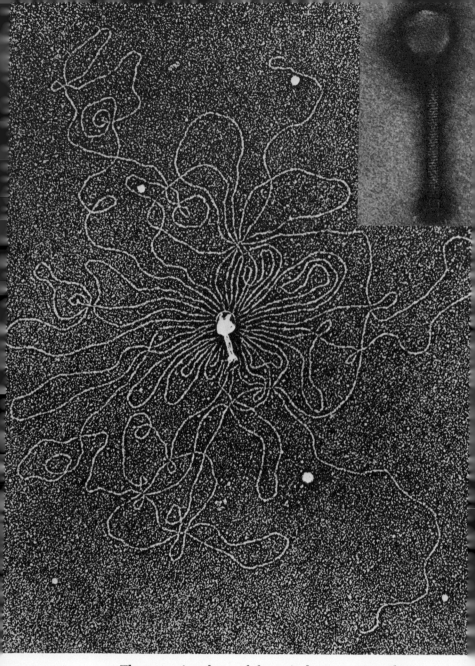

Electron microphoto of bacteriophage, a virus that preys on bacteria. In the large picture the virus has been chemically "shocked" into releasing its DNA into the surrounding medium. The insert shows the virus with the DNA packed into the head. Length of the virus is about 0.2 micron.

Since viruses have this property, and are highly specific in the tissues they infect, it has been suggested that the tables be turned and that they be put to work in the service of man. Scientists are finding that viruses can be modified or even synthesized to have specific properties. Suppose, for instance, we were dealing with a defect involving lack of a specific enzyme. Perhaps a virus could be designed that would contain instructions to the cell to produce the missing substance. The patient could then be "vaccinated" with the virus, which would multiply in the body and cause it to produce the needed enzyme.

It is even conceivable that such a treatment may be used one day in the future to reverse the effects of aging. We turn now to that subject, with which every single one of us is directly concerned.

5

Aging and the Importance of Death

AGING CAN BE looked at as a disease. Everyone has it, and it is 100 per cent fatal. But he who asks for cure had better be careful how he asks. The Greeks understood this. In one of their myths Eos, goddess of the dawn, falls in love with Tithonus, a mortal man. Since she, being a goddess, would live forever, she asks Zeus, god of all gods, for immortality for Tithonus. This he grants.

Nevertheless, to her surprise and chagrin, Tithonus shortly begins to age and become infirm. Too late she realizes her mistake. She had forgotten that immortality for her meant eternal youth, which she had neglected to specifically include in her request for Tithonus. His immortality is therefore to be one of eternal old age. This was hardly what Eos had in mind. Eventually she confines him to chamber from which only his voice can be heard. And finally she turns him into a cricket.

The story is more than two thousand years old, yet it has perfect relevance today. Some of the medical techniques we have already mentioned (such as transplants) will keep someone alive who might ordinarily have died, but it will not keep him young. We still have not found a cure for aging.

The search for eternal, or at least extended, youth has gone on for thousands of years. In most cases of past "treatments," some form of magic was involved. Dr. Faust signed a pact with the devil. Ponce de León sought a mythical, magical Fountain of Youth. The Babylonian hero Gilgamesh went through all kinds of adventures in his search for eternal youth; he finally came up with a magic plant that would restore youth to an old man, but it was unfortunately stolen by a serpent. And so on.

Various kinds of chemical treatments were also suggested. Paracelsus, the founder of modern chemistry, had his Mercury of Life, and Francis Bacon, who some would call the father of modern science, suggested treatments that included the use of precious and semiprecious gems, gold, and the "heart-bone of a deer." The Roman Pliny suggested eating Caucasian monkeys that had eaten a lot of pepper.

As far as we know, none of these ideas worked.

We could look to someone who has accomplished the feat of remaining alive for ninety or one hundred years. Clearly he or she would be an expert on the subject. Thus anyone whose age has begun to creep up into the nineties is sure to have been asked many times, "What is your secret?" The answers have ranged all the way from, "Plenty of rest, fresh air, and good food," to "A pint of whiskey a day." It undoubtedly never occurred to the one who gives the second answer that he may have lived as long as he did, not *because* of his "secret," but *in spite of it.* It is still safe to say that your best bet for a long life is to choose parents and grandparents who are long-lived.

If all four of your grandparents lived to eighty or beyond, you are likely to live four years longer than average. (Today the average life expectancy of someone living in a Western country is some seventy years.)

But if you do not come from a long-lived line, don't despair. Environment also plays an important part. Indeed, if you live

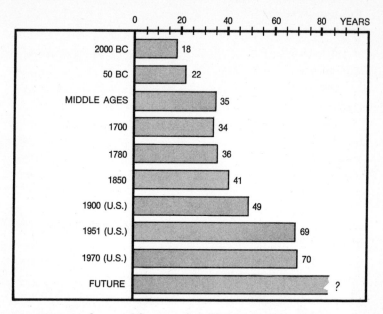

Average human life span through history. Note jump from 1900 to 1951 as a result of medical advances.

in the country, you are likely to live several years longer than a city dweller. And the one who lives in a big city seems to have the edge, all other things being equal, over the one who lives in a small town.

Modern medicine, plus a greater and wider selection of foods, seems to have made most of us larger as well as healthier than our parents and grandparents. The average height of Americans has increased at something like an inch per generation. And the average age of Americans and those in other technically advanced countries has also gone up.

This is deceptive, however. It does not mean that a greater percentage of us are living to see the age of one hundred. In ancient Greece alone, Epimenides, Democritus, Isocrates, Zeno, Thales, Xenophon, and Apollonias were all said to have lived to one hundred or beyond. Even if we assume that not all of these men really lived that long, remember that this was at a time when the average life span was twenty-two. As a matter of fact, for reasons we will give later, it may be that less people today (in proportion to total numbers) live to the century mark. An old man is still old.

What the higher average life span of today does mean is that fewer of us are dying at early ages from various diseases. What we really want, in terms of aging, is a bonus of five, ten, or even fifty years between the ages of twenty and thirty, that is, a slowing of the aging process.

As we suggested just above, it may even be that an over-abundance of good food has an adverse effect on longevity. Clearly it has not been possible to perform scientific experiments on humans, but work with smaller mammals does seem to point in this direction.

In the 1930's, Dr. Clive M. McCay of Cornell University performed a classic experiment that has intrigued students of aging ever since. Here is how it came about. A common idea about aging is that the process begins when we stop growing, roughly at ages eighteen to twenty. The turtle, perhaps the only animal that can outlive man, appears to accomplish this by continuing to grow indefinitely. A few fish, such as the carp, the plaice, and the sturgeon, can also grow all their lives; they thereby live longer than others which do not, though not as long as man. Some trees, too, seem to have the ability to just keep on growing. A few, notably the redwoods and the bristlecone pine, can live for several *thousand* years.

All mammals, however, seem to reach some definite size, at which point their bones harden into final form. After that time, the operation of the body is such that it merely replaces dead and dying cells (except for nerve cells in the central nervous system which are not replaced). And even dead cells are not replaced perfectly. We can be sure of this because if it were not true, there would be no aging.

McCay wondered what would happen if a mammal were

prevented from "growing up." One way to do this, he reasoned, would be to provide only enough food to the animal for it to perform its living functions, but not enough for it to add to its size. He chose as subjects rats with a normal life span of about three years. The test rats were raised on a restricted diet, while the control group was fed a normal diet. Summarizing the results, it was found that the test rats were still growing while the control rats had already reached maturity or even died. In some cases, the life span was in effect doubled. I would not recommend that you try this method, however. What works on rats does not necessarily work on humans; children brought up on inadequate diets have been found to develop numerous problems, including some mental retardation. Further, the test rats were also found to have osteoporosis—fragile bones—a disease common in old people.

What McCay did show very neatly, however, is that the maximum age of a creature is apparently not fixed.

Aside from magic and variation in food, then, what else can be done to increase longevity? Over the ages, it is likely that thousands of methods have been tried. Not one, obviously, has done the trick. Or, if someone knows the secret, he is keeping it to himself.

Two 900-day old rats show aging differences resulting from different diets. Senile rat on left was fed unrestricted diet. Diet of younger-looking rat was nutritionally adequate but restricted. Experiment was performed by Dr. Clive M. McCay at Cornell University in the 1930's.

Theories of Aging

We said before that with understanding comes control. Turning this around, we realize that control requires understanding. What, then, do we know about aging? Not a great deal. We do not really know what it is, let alone how to cure or prevent it. Indeed, even some of the hard evidence obtained by experimentation seems to be conflicting. The basic question might be phrased thus: Do cells have a built-in life span, or is the environment in which they live the determining factor? McCay's work points in the latter direction, that there is no built-in timer. So does an experiment performed by a French-American surgeon, Alexis Carrel. He kept a piece of chicken heart alive for thirty-four years, far longer than the normal life span of a whole chicken.

Dr. Alexis Carrel kept a piece of chicken heart alive for thirty-four years, some ten times the normal life span of a chicken.

Yet, other work contradicts this idea. There are cases of identical twins who, though living apart, died of the same cause at the same time. And Professor Leonard Hayflick, now with the Stanford University School of Medicine, has found evidence that human cells, at least, do have a built-in clock of some sort. In experiments, he found that normal animal cells in a culture medium cannot be made to reproduce themselves more than about fifty times. In his work, this meant a life of only about six to eight months.

Referring to Carrel's work and other work with laboratory mice that pointed to the idea of no built-in times, he says that "if care is taken not to add any living cells to the initial population [of cells] in the glass vessel, the cell colony will not survive long. The early cultures, including Carrel's, were fed a crude extract taken from chick embryos, and it is now believed that these feedings must have contained some living chick cells. That is to say, in all probability the reason the cultures continued to grow indefinitely was that new, viable fibroblasts were introduced into the culture at each feeding." *

Under certain conditions, it has been found, cells will "transform" and will apparently lose the built-in division limit; but they are no longer normal cells, for they take on cancer-like properties.

This and other evidence suggests at least some connection between cancer and aging. Indeed, one of the leading theories of aging involves the same basic idea as that of cancer, namely, that something eventually goes wrong with the information being transferred from parent to daughter cells. Just as the rubber mold an artist might use to make a number of reproductions of his original might begin to get fuzzy about the edges, so too might the DNA of dividing cells become blurred with an accumulation of copying errors. This leads to changes or inabilities in the functioning of

* "Human Cells and Aging," L. Hayflick, p. 32.

enzymes, which shows itself as a reduced capacity of the organism as a whole.

One possible cause is the natural radiation to which all of us are exposed through our lives. This radiation comes from cosmic rays that are blasting their way into our atmosphere at all times, from radioactivity in the earth, from the use of X-rays and radioactive materials in medicine and industry, and other causes. (This brings up an interesting question. Suppose you knew that you could lengthen your life span by ten years by wearing a ten-pound suit of radiation-proof armor for the rest of your life. Would you do it?)

Still within the information-loss theory, there is the additional possibility that our bodies fall victim to our own disease-fighting (immunity) apparatus. Our antibodies, for instance, might no longer recognize parts of our body as our own and might begin to attack them as they would foreign transplants.

Another theory has to do with the continued accumulation in the body of certain unwanted chemical substances. Or perhaps there is a loss of certain needed chemicals because of the general slowing down of the body processes in aging.

There might also be a gradual chemical cross-linking of various proteins in the body—in the same way that certain materials such as soft rubber get hard and stiff with aging. This would not only cause a physical handicap, but would also impair the delivery of nutrients, oxygen, and chemical messages (hormones) to and from various parts of the body. And it certainly has been found that certain tissues in aging bodies, such as muscle, are slowly replaced by stiff connecting tissue.

But is this a cause or a result of aging? Baldness too is a sign of aging, but no one has ever claimed it as a cause. Nevertheless, it may be possible to break down these cross-links so as to restore or maintain the original resiliency.

Treatment for Aging

The fact that women, on the average, live longer than men —some seven years longer in the United States—has never been satisfactorily explained. It would seem, however, that hormones are somehow implicated. It is also known that the sex hormones play an important part in the maturation (development) of men and women; thus it has often been thought that these, particularly, might be useful in somehow combating the aging process. As long ago as 1889, a 72-year-old man by the name of Brown-Sequard had himself injected with abstracts from the testicles of young animals in hopes that this would rejuvenate him. Although the results are not entirely clear, it is said that he did indeed experience some increase of youth and vigor, although not for very long.

There have been revivals of such treatments from time to time—always advertised as *the* answer to the problem of aging. Quite obviously, however, their efficacy as a general treatment has never been satisfactorily proved. Further, serious side effects often arise when one begins to alter the glandular and hormonal balance of the body. Although hormone treatment for the aged, such as estrogen for women and testosterone for men, is fairly common today, it is used not so much as a way of retarding aging but as treatment for the various imbalances that aging brings about. Still, the various hormones are involved in the aging process and will undoubtedly be useful and more widely used later on as experience accumulates.

One intriguing discovery, called "juvenile hormone," keeps insects from moving into their next stage. That is to say, if they are given juvenile hormone while in the larval stage, they will not metamorphose into the next, or pupal stage. Is there

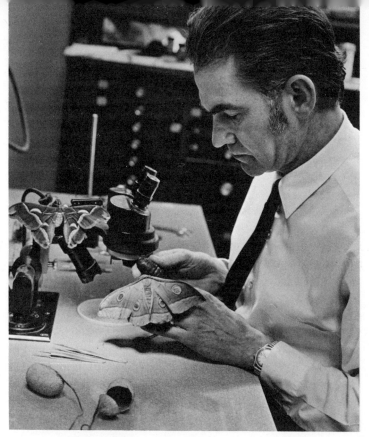

Dr. Carroll Williams of Harvard University, one of the pioneers in juvenile hormones, examines various stages in the life cycle of a giant moth.

some analogous substance that would keep humans from moving from prime to middle years? Perhaps.

Are there any other ways to slow up the aging process? Yes. The normal life of the stickleback fish is some fourteen to eighteen months. One investigator showed that in subpolar regions it takes several years before they even become sexually mature, while in warmer waters this takes place in a few months. Similarly, it has been observed that the life span of sardines increases with higher latitude.

At first thought one might therefore expect that Eskimos live longer than Africans. But humans are mammals, not fish, and are warm-blooded. Thus their body temperature does not change with outside temperature. Nevertheless, it has been calculated that reducing the body temperature by a mere three degrees would add twenty years of life to the average man. Drugs that can reduce body temperature have already been developed.

What's the catch? Merely that everything, not just aging, would slow down; for chemical reaction time is directly proportional to temperature. Fast reaction time in a cool climate was the greatest advantage that the mammal had over the reptile during the mammal's early years of development. It was able to maintain a constant, and relatively high, body temperature and was therefore able to move fast in weather that slowed down the larger, more vicious reptiles.

Is this ability as important today? While physical speed is no longer an absolute necessity (except for crossing some streets), mental ability certainly is. So the main problem with reducing body temperature is that the brain would slow down too. Not only would there be no more four-minute miles, but probably no more Einsteins or Beethovens either. Perhaps we could develop new and more potent enzymes that would permit equivalent or even faster chemical reaction times while at the same time permitting a reduction in temperature. But the body is such a delicately balanced instrument that this seems a rather unlikely possibility.

You have probably realized that the cooling we have been talking about often presents itself in the form of hibernation, which is really quite common in nature, but which is actually an adaptation to cold weather. Perhaps it could be arranged that we hibernate at night in place of sleeping, which would probably add some years to our lives. On the other hand, the organs in our bodies are still working, cleaning out wastes, building tissue, and so on, while we sleep. Slowing down these processes might be harmful in the long run.

But how about going a step further, namely, suspended animation, in which the processes are not just slowed down but are stopped entirely. In an interesting book called *The Prospect of Immortality*, R. C. W. Ettinger points out, rightly, how strange it is that "popular articles on suspended animation have mentioned chiefly its possible use by astronauts on long interstellar voyages! This aspect is trivial. Its importance lies not in travel to the stars, for the few, but in travel to the future, for the many."

To put it simply, Ettinger and others propose nothing less than the freezing of the recently dead, or even the sick and aged, until such time as society has licked the medical or physical problem involved. At that time, the body would be "defrosted," the malady treated, and the person involved put back into a full, satisfying life by the advanced medical procedures then in force.

While this sounds ridiculous at first, we must maintain an open mind. Who would have believed, a century ago, that man would walk on the moon? Certain simple life forms can go into a state of suspended animation through the simple process of drying out or freezing. A bit of moisture or warmth is all that is needed to bring them back to life. Further, some small animals and even certain kinds of human tissue have been successfully frozen and brought back to life. There are also cases of humans whose body temperature has dropped twenty degrees or more and who have come back to life.

It is also true that very few people, perhaps none, die of old age. Almost invariably there is a specific cause of death, or perhaps more than one. Thus the medical team of the future may need "only" to treat a kidney disease, or a massive heart attack, after they have brought the body back to life.

Ettinger admits, by the way, that this small matter, "defrosting," has not really been figured out yet; but he feels that it is only a matter of time. Things like damage to cell

75

walls by freezing of body fluids can be handled, he is sure. Or substances like glycerol can be injected which will act as an antifreeze.

He is confident, furthermore, that any damage that is done can be repaired. Consider, for example, damage to the brain, the one type of damage that most physicians consider irreparable. Ettinger writes, "It is not inconceivable that huge surgeon-machines, working twenty-four hours a day for decades or even centuries, will tenderly restore the frozen brains, cell by cell, or even molecule by molecule in critical areas."

Not inconceivable, but pretty nearly so.

There is another small problem. In a world that will probably be even more densely populated than it is today, who will want these frozen people? Will the society, no doubt with serious problems of its own, really be willing to do all the work necessary to defrost them, cure them of whatever ailed them, and provide the necessary training and sympathetic handling that would be necessary to bring them into harmony with the new age? One or two, perhaps a dozen. But as a large-scale project?

Nevertheless, it should be pointed out that not one but several groups, dedicated to this idea, have been formed. The Cryonics Society of New York alone already has four persons deep-frozen in its vaults.

Should the process be made to work, man would truly have gained a way to travel into the future. It is interesting to note that our own Ben Franklin dreamed of doing this very thing. He was even given an idea of how to do it when he noted that flies sometimes seemed to drown in wine but would revive when placed in the sun. When he was in his late sixties he wrote, with characteristic playfulness, to a friend:

Having a very ardent desire to see and observe the state of America a hundred years hence, I should prefer to any

ordinary death the being immersed in a cask of Madeira wine
with a few friends til that time, to be then recalled to life by
the solar warmth of my dear country.

Long Life Can Create Problems

Let us now make the grand leap and suppose that aging has
been licked, that we can now live, say, five hundred years.
Wouldn't that be wonderful? Well, it might be if you and I
and a few others were the only ones. But if everyone was able
to live to the age of five hundred, the effects on society would
be extraordinary. If you think it is difficult to get changes
made now, what do you suppose would happen when the same
people are in power for hundreds of years? And if you think
they would be willing to relinquish the reins after fifty or so
years, so they can vegetate for four centuries, you're wrong.

Under the best of conditions they will have been given
extended prime years, not old age. Will they continue to pro-
create for several hundred years, producing thirty or forty
children per couple?

We are, in other words, playing with fire. No one (or almost
no one) is urging that work along these lines be stopped. But
we must surely be very careful. We may be creating a monster.

The one claim that can sensibly be made for longer life,
aside from appeasing our naturally selfish motives, would be
that we would have time to become wiser. To the objection
that 90-year-olds have not in general been twice as wise as
they were at 45, there is the answer that they were already
declining and losing brain power at 45. Would an additional
half century or more of "prime time" really make a difference?
It is conceivable. My own feeling is that it would not, that
even if mental power and wisdom go up, enthusiasm and
staying power would go down. Further, Nobel Prize winner
George Wald points out that even if aging were licked, "all
the other ills that flesh is heir to would remain—disease, war,

77

IN THE WORLD OF THE FUTURE

traffic accidents, accidents of all sorts." Some even feel that man would become so worried about his big bundle of years that he would stop taking any chances. He would become a miser, as sometimes happens to one who becomes rich. General society might very well suffer thereby.

The Importance of Death

In a science fiction story called *The City and the Stars,* by Arthur C. Clarke, two groups of intelligent beings inhabit the same planet but are completely separated geographically and have nothing to do with one another. One group is mortal, as we are. The other is immortal and, in a manner not too different from Ettinger's proposal, some fraction of the group are put into prolonged sleep at specific times. To put it another way, they take turns living. They have to, for they have reached the limits of population growth.

The members of this group are of a very high order and live very comfortably. But a visitor to this section from the other finds something very interesting. There are no children. There cannot be. The society has thereby become ossified, hardened into a form without change, and without possibility of change.

I won't give away the rest of the story, or the ending, which is an interesting one. But consider whether you would want to live in such a society.

Not only society, but human beings as a species might also suffer. That we are humans and not monkeys or worms or even protozoa we owe to this process called death. Some protozoa, like amoeba, live forever. They simply divide and keep on dividing as long as their environment is satisfactory. But they remain protozoa and are probably no different than they were billions of years ago. This is because the "old ones" do not die after an appointed time, but in effect hang around forever, thus preventing change from taking place.

Aging and the
Importance of Death

Animals on a somewhat higher scale, such as insects and crustaceans, possess remarkable powers of regeneration, but they all die. The higher the degree of specialization, the less are the powers of regeneration and immortality. Or so it seems so far. Wald puts it this way: "Death as the inevitable conclusion to life appears to have been a late invention in evolution. One can go a long way up the scale of living organisms without having to encounter a corpse." Reproduction by division, he points out, can be found among animals as complex as sea anemones and worms.

But to have gotten higher up on the scale, it seems, death had to be introduced into the world. It may well be the price we had to pay to become really complex creatures.

The slow-growing Bristlecone Pine can live for several thousand years.

Another way of looking at the question is this. Man has evolved from the lower animals by the twin processes of mutation and natural selection. Mutation, as you know, means a change in the hereditary material, the DNA, of the cell. Natural selection refers to the fact that in nature animals compete for survival, not necessarily through battle, but in all kinds of ways, such as obtaining enough water, food, and living space. The important time of the "choosing," however, is *before* the age of reproduction. For if the animal lives until then, he can pass on his traits, good or bad, to his offspring. Normally, however, any defects he may have had that would have made him less capable of surviving would have been weeded out by his being killed before he reproduced. What happened to him after reproduction did not affect the laws of evolution at all.

We have, in more senses than one, fallen in love with our bodies. Our long lives have made this possible. But to nature, our bodies are dispensable. It is the germ plasm that is important. Our bodies are merely the bridges from one egg cell to another. Or as someone put it, "A hen is merely an egg's way of producing another egg."

Man, as a species, would continue even if everyone died immediately after reproduction. This is literally true of the salmon, the eel, and the lamprey. For them, reproduction is the last act of life. The Pacific salmon, for example, advances from youth to old age in the two weeks or so that it takes for it to head up into the island rivers to spawn. During that time, remarkable changes occur in its body, one being that its digestive system collapses and it simply stops eating. When it has completed its migration and reproductive act, there is nothing left for it but to die.

Perhaps, by analogy, it would be best if a good age span could be figured out for man, during all of which he remained young and strong. Then all of his aging would take place during the last few days of his life.

6

Creating Life

THE GRAND MARCH of science—which often involves an about-face or two—has perhaps never been better illustrated than in the story of *spontaneous generation*. Spontaneous generation is a long term for a simple idea, namely, that living things can arise out of non-living material.

For thousands of years it was "common knowledge" that flies can arise from rotting meat as well as from parent flies. The basic idea was that the fermenting or putrefaction process, i.e., the rotting, somehow did the trick.

In 1667 a well-known Flemish physician and scientist, J. B. van Helmont, gave this recipe for making mice: ". . . if you put a piece of underwear soiled with sweat together with some wheat in an open-mouth jar, after about twenty-one days the odor changes and the ferment, coming out of the underwear and penetrating through the husks of the wheat, changes the wheat into mice."

How could anyone doubt this? All one had to do was try it, and sure enough the mice would appear. Isn't this the true test of a theory? Yes, but one must also, as I am sure you appreciate, prevent external factors from interfering with, and influencing, the experiment. One of the first to appreciate this was Francesco Redi, an Italian physician and poet. Only a year after van Helmont published his recipe, Redi decided to challenge the basic idea of spontaneous generation, but he worked with rotting meat and flies. Basically what he did was put fresh meat into jars; one he left open and the other he protected with a muslin screen.

After a few days, he found both eggs and larvae (an intermediate stage between eggs and adult flies) on the meat in the open jar. He found some eggs on the muslin that was protecting the meat in the second jar, but none in the meat itself. What had happened was clear. Adult flies, attracted by the rotting meat, had simply laid eggs on it. Obvious, when someone finally thought to approach the problem properly.

The question of the spontaneous generation of microorganisms was attacked and laid to rest in a smiliar manner by the great French chemist Louis Pasteur. Pasteur was then to write, "Never will the doctrine of spontaneous generation recover from the mortal blow of this simple experiment."

Life, Pasteur had clearly shown, can only arise from life. But, if this is so, how, and where, *did* life first arise? This

Pasteur showed that fermentation or putrefaction results from the action of airborne organisms. Culture broth in flask at left remains clear because airborne organisms are trapped in S-curve of neck. If neck is severed as shown at right, organisms can reach broth and putrefaction takes place.

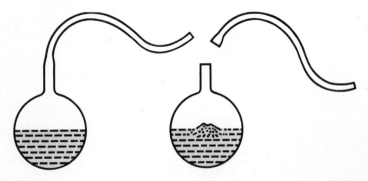

is a question that Pasteur chose (wisely) to ignore, but it has plagued scientists and philosophers for thousands of years. Mythical explanations have been common for a long time.

Myths are traditional stories that generally concern supernatural events and gods. Some are funny (to us), some are sad, some are simple-minded, many are quite complex. All attempt the same: to explain, usually in story form, some aspect of nature or history. Among the best known are the Greek myths, which gave names and human forms to such things as lightning and thunder, love and war, the sun and the moon.

In other words, what a myth does is "explain" something or some activity by anthropomorphizing (or humanizing) it. It is the human (or god) that is causing the natural phenomenon to happen. For example, the sun chariot was *driven* across the sky at dawn each day by Apollo, who was, among other things, the Greek god of the sun.

This giving of animate reasons for inanimate occurrences leads to some interesting possibilities. Thus the statement "sunrise follows dawn" could be restated as "Apollo pursues Daphne." The second statement has quite a different meaning from the first.

Virtually every human group has its myths of creation— the creation of the universe, of the sun, of the earth, of life. The story of Genesis in the Bible is the best-known example (to the Western world) of a creation myth: "And God said, Let the earth bring forth the living creature after its kind, cattle and creeping thing, and beast of the earth. . . ."

The creation myth in the Hindu religion is a little more specific, and uses a fairly common creation idea, that of the egg. Out of a dark, swirling, hot sea there one day appeared a golden egg. After a long time the egg split in half. The upper half became the heavens, the lower half the earth, while in between the air and the clouds formed. Out of the egg too came all the creatures and living things of the earth.

These were imaginative attempts, the best that could be done at the time. They may be impressive or fun to read, but modern science does not find very much in them to work with, and a whole new group of explanations has arisen. Of course, some future group, studying the science of the twentieth century, may chuckle at *our* attempts to explain the origins of life, for we too may be all wrong. Nevertheless, there is a basic difference between early attempts to explain the origins of earth and ours: The early myths did not contain within them the possibility of test to see if they made scientific sense.

I use the term *scientific* advisedly. For the early explanations did make sense, at least to the people of the time. The Greeks maintained that the chief god, Zeus, threw lightning bolts when he was angry at something man did. Well, it was as good an explanation of lightning as any at the time. The problem with it as a scientific explanation is that there is no way to test it.

In general, *our* "myths" are testable. Indeed, a scientific theory is only considered useful if it can be tested. In spite of Redi and Pasteur, for example, it is commonly believed among scientists today that life could have arisen from non-life—*abiogenetically*—without the intervention of a god or other supernatural creator.

But it is one thing to make such a statement, and another to be able to prove it. Unfortunately, testing cannot always be as simple and straightforward as Redi's and Pasteur's. It would be nice (if a bit frightening) if one could simply pour a couple of chemicals into a flask and come up with a worm or hamster. No one can do that now, and it is highly unlikely that anyone will ever be able to do it.

For one thing, we may look at a maze of wires in a telephone circuit or a computer and marvel at its complexity, and at the fact that man can create, or build, something as complex as that. But compared with even a "simple" one-celled creature, they are simplicity itself. Indeed, anything that man has created, whatever it may be, is still far, far simpler than even the simplest living cell. And multicelled creatures are yet another order of magnitude more complicated. Even nature cannot create a multicelled creature from scratch. Every complex, or "higher," organism, no matter how large, starts life as a single cell.

Nor can nature create even a single cell from scratch, i.e., as a mixture of chemical substances. We may not know the secret of life, but we are very sure of this. The living cell is just as far, in evolutionary terms, from inanimate matter, as we are from the one-celled creature.

And, finally, the conditions on earth today are very different from what they were before life began on earth. This is not only a case of the passage of time and, say, normal wear and tear on the earth and its atmosphere. No, earth and life have evolved together over the eons of time.

So to challenge a scientist to produce a living thing in a flask is to challenge him to do something that even nature could not do now.

What the scientist can do, and is attempting to do, is to re-create some of, or perhaps all the steps (including changes in the conditions of life on earth) that were taken in the building of life forms. These steps have taken nature several billions of years. Man's experimental attempts go back less than half a century.

Nevertheless, he has accomplished quite a bit in that short time. Let us look at some of his experiments, and at some possibilities for the future.

Experimental Approach

We have just mentioned that earth and life had evolved together over eons of time. This is particularly true of our atmosphere. It is now generally believed that most of the oxygen in our atmosphere, so necessary to the survival of animal life, has been generated by plant life only since the process of photosynthesis came into being. And photosynthesis, it turns out, is a relatively late evolutionary development.

What, then, was the primitive atmosphere like? This question was to prove extraordinarily fruitful in the earch for the origins of life.

It was the American chemist and Nobel Prize winner Harold C. Urey who suggested, in the early 1950's, that the early atmosphere of the earth was nothing like it is today.

Instead of being oxygen- and nitrogen-filled, the early atmosphere probably consisted largely of hydrogen, ammonia, and methane—thoroughly poisonous to animal life but, interestingly, similar to the atmospheres of the large outer planets today.

With this idea there arose a possible experimental approach. Before we discuss it, however, let us look for a moment at a question that is closely related to the question of the origin of life: What *is* life? The vitalists, remember, say that some unknown force is involved in life. The mechanists claim that it is only necessary to put the proper chemicals together in the proper way and under the proper conditions, and that life will arise spontaneously. Now, one of the basic properties of living things is that, driven by some form of energy, they become both larger and more complex. In the case of plants, this energy is derived directly from the sun by photosynthesis; animals depend upon chemical energy stored in the tissues of plants or other animals.

Indeed, say the mechanists, the basic difference between living and non-living things is one of organization. Living things tend to be more complex; aside from that there is no basic difference. Elemental substances like carbon, oxygen, and hydrogen are built into amino acids, which in turn are built into proteins, which in turn are built into tissues, and so on.

On the other hand, the natural tendency of non-living things is to *break down* with the passage of time and application of energy—as boulders are weathered into pebbles and sand by wind, rain, and sun, and cars are reduced to piles of rusty junk.

If the mechanists are right, then it should be possible to cause basic organic materials to come together into more complex forms.

It was believed that life had originally formed in the oceans or other bodies of water. All the earliest fossils, dating from one half to one billion years ago, are from water-dwelling creatures.

Urey mulled over these things, and an experiment began to form in his mind. What, he wondered, would happen if the proposed constitutents of the primitive atmosphere were put together into a flask with carefully purified and sterilized water, and the whole subjected to some form of energy? Would the separate constituents come together and build up into a more highly organized state?

Dr. Stanley Miller, at the time a student of Urey's, performed the experiment and reported the results in 1953. Perhaps you can imagine the reaction of other scientists when they learned that upon opening the flask and examining the contents, Miller found some amino acids!

Amino acids, the building blocks of proteins, are normally never found in non-living things; yet they had been built up from totally and completely inanimate substances—and in only a week.

Those who had quietly and studiously been pondering the philosophical question, "What is life?" were pulled to attention. Since then other workers have been able to synthesize proteins, enzymes, and nucleic acids.

Does this mean that life has been created in a test tube? Not a single reputable scientist would go so far as to say so. Professor A. I. Oparin, one of the first workers in the field,

87

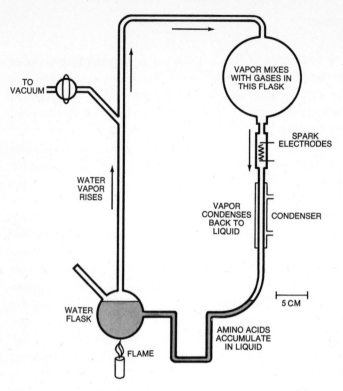

Apparatus used by Dr. Stanley Miller to synthesize amino acids.

wrote in his world-renowned book, *Life: Its Nature, Origin and Development,* ". . . any attempt at the direct, artificial reproduction or synthesis of even the simplest of living things must still be regarded as naive."

What we *have* seen is evidence that under the proper conditions, non-living things will apparently link together into higher patterns of organization. But then an obvious question arises. Why then does not life continually arise anew? The answer is easily given: Because life has already arisen and, consisting as it does of predators of all kinds and at all levels, it will promptly gobble up any organic materials that might otherwise be on their way toward life.

In earliest times, however, conditions were much better for

the development of life in many ways. As mentioned, there were no predators around. Secondly, there were good raw materials in abundance. The British geneticist J. B. S. Haldane suggests that, at least in places, the waters of the earth at the time may have been a kind of hot, dilute "soup."

The lack of oxygen may actually have been useful. Today the oxygen in the atmosphere forms a layer some ten to twenty miles up that filters out much of the ultraviolet light from the sun's rays. Too much ultraviolet light is deadly to living things. In the early days, however, ultraviolet radiation, along with lightning, atmospheric electricity, radioactive materials in the earth, cosmic rays, and so on, were probably all instrumental in getting the process of life started. They may also have kept it going until other, more advanced forms of obtaining energy were developed. These other forms include photosynthesis, respiration, and utilization of the chemical energy stored up by plants by means of photosynthesis. The British astronomer and writer V. A. Firsoff suggests that the beginnings of life may have been something like a virus infection spreading through Haldane's "soup."

These various compounds that were forming were of course nothing like the life, even microscopic life, with which we are familiar now. They were disorganized, did not reproduce, and did not respond to variations in their surroundings. For, as Professor Oparin has pointed out, ". . . life is not simply scattered about all over the place, but only exists in individual organisms which are separate from their environment."

Experiments run since Miller's have shown that natural laws will cause a number of life-like processes to take place automatically. Just as oil in water will, when shaken, form separate droplets, so too might these compounds have formed into separate cells under the action of waves. The walls of the various cells could have had a natural beginning in the purely physical idea of surface tension. Try dropping a needle or razor blade gently (and not edge first) onto the surface of a container of water. Not only will the metal object float, but if you look carefully, you will see that the water is actually dented by the object. The surface, in other words, has formed a "skin." Not only that, but such a skin will, depending upon what is inside a drop it encloses, actually permit certain molecules to enter, while keeping others out. It becomes, in other words, a semi-permeable membrane, just as our cell walls are.

Even more realistically, it has been found that substances of high molecular weight (the hallmark of living things), such as proteins, will spontaneously clump together and form separate droplets when placed in water. It has been shown that these small spheres, sometimes called *coacervates,* will do some interesting things. In one experiment the coacervate absorbed glucose and gave out maltose. This kind of process, the production of something quite different from itself out of substances surrounding the object, is another important characteristic of living things.

Still another is reproduction. Oparin suggested many years ago that the earliest growing coacervates might have been divided in some way by external action, as by the action of breaking waves.

But this may not even have been necessary. A growing droplet may very well divide automatically because of the natural laws governing surface tension, volume vs. weight, molecular electric effects, and so on. Dr. Sidney W. Fox of the University of Miami in Florida, for example, has obtained protein-like materials by heating amino acids, which caused them to link together. Dr. Fox calls them *proteinoid* (protein-like) microspheres; they have been shown to have a number of weak enzyme-like, i.e., catalytic, activities, and a number of other properties of typical proteins as well. Perhaps the most extraordinary characteristic of Fox's microspheres is that they are quite stable, but will, after a week or so, bud in a manner reminiscent of the reproduction of yeast cells. This is shown in the illustration.

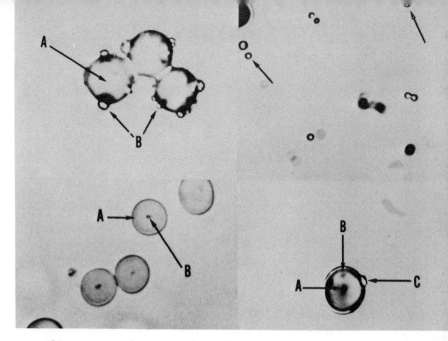

This sequence shows a cycle in the "life" of a man-made proteinoid (protein-like) microspheres. At top left, the microspheres (A) can be seen budding (B) as some yeasts and bacteria do. The buds are shown at top right after they have broken away from the "parents" (with help from the experimenter). At lower left, new microspheres (A) have grown around the buds. At lower right, the process is beginning again.

Another extraordinary phenomenon that must have been in evidence over the billions of years in question is Darwin's process of evolution. That is to say, those types of molecules that worked best and lived longest in their environment were the ones that got most of whatever nourishment there was.

Perhaps you find this difficult to accept, since evolution is normally thought of only in connection with living things. But there seems little doubt that a process of natural selection was taking place in this pre-life world as well. Why is this any harder to believe than that something as complex as a human being developed in a similar manner out of the unicellular creatures that were the only inhabitants of the earth some billions of years ago?

The Step to Life?

By this time you are probably wondering when we will finally get to the point where life actually arose on earth. In other words, somewhere, at some time, the step to life must have been taken. The vitalist is particularly interested in this point, for it is here that the entry of the "vital force" must be at least considered.

But no, life is not that simple. There is no one point or dividing line on one side of which we have life and on the other, non-life. For on the ladder we are using to climb the wall of life, there are a number of steps along the way at which life-like properties are exhibited by non-living things.

The point of the question, of course, is how will we know when we have created life in a test tube? Believe it or not, it is just possible that we will not know. For one thing, it has not even been possible for agreement to be reached on a workable definition of life, and particularly one that would permit an unambiguous distinction between life and non-life. Try it. Look up the defintion of life in a few references —dictionaries, biology books—and see whether you can come up with a satisfactory distinction between animate and inanimate matter. There is still no agreement, for instance, as to whether to call viruses living things. Nor do we fully know the chemistry of a living cell.

Each of the basic processes of life—such as growth, metabolism, and reproduction—has its counterpart in non-living matter. A common example is the growth of a crystal. It is only when all come together, and work together, that the thing we call life is suddenly recognizable.

We get little help in our search from the fossil record. The fossil evidence of early life is pretty good back to about 500 million years ago, not nearly as good, but in existence, back to 1 billion years ago. Before that we can see nothing. Yet the fossils we have found are complex enough to indicate that there must have been a long period of development before then, perhaps as much as another 2 billion years. It may well be that there were many abortive starts, both in time and place, before life really took hold.

Or consider the problem of whether plants or animals arose first. Animals, somewhere along the line, depend upon plants for their existence, and so it would seem that plants developed first. But it is known that photosynthesis, the basic process by which plants use sunlight to convert hydrogen, oxygen, and carbon into food, did not arise until much later. Therefore it is quite likely that the first living things were a kind of animal predator, the "prey" being the simple organic substances in the dilute "soup" of Haldane's.

It has been suggested that the first "true" living organism was a short stretch of DNA, just long enough to cause the production of an enzyme. But even the production of an enzyme requires such complex chemistry that the sophisticated structuring of DNA could only have been a relatively recent development.

We have come nowhere near matching the complexity of nucleic acids in laboratory experiments with primeval atmospheres.

Fortunately, there are other approaches. Professor Sol Spiegelman, now with Columbia University, has already produced self-replicating RNA in the laboratory. In this work, done in 1965 at the University of Illinois, he started with RNA that he obtained from a virus. Then, using this RNA as a template or pattern, he was able to keep producing new viruses by adding chemicals to a solution containing magnesium and an enzyme.

In 1967 Dr. Arthur Kornberg and a team of researchers at the Stanford University School of Medicine synthesized viral DNA rings that were capable of reproducing themselves.

In the illustration, each closed loop is a complete double

helix. One strand of each loop is a natural single strand of a bacterial virus, which served as a template for the test-tube synthesis of an artificial complementary strand.

Professor Spiegelman points out that the major value of this type of work is that reproduction of genes can now be studied under controlled laboratory conditions, rather than in the far more complicated world of living cells. The work also demonstrates the ability to manipulate the genetic code.

Looking at this type of work in another way, we see clearly that no science, theoretical or experimental, operates in a vacuum. Almost every development is adapted and finds use elsewhere. This type of synthesis is no exception. In a more recent application, a synthetic double-stranded RNA was used on an infectious DNA virus known as *Herpes simplex*. This is a virus which normally causes cold sores in man, but which sometimes causes blindness and even death. Certain other

Electron micrograph of DNA synthesized in a test tube by Dr. Arthur Kornberg and others at the Stanford University School of Medicine. Each of these closed loops of DNA is a complete double helix containing about 5500 pairs of bases. Diameter of the outside loop is about two microns (or two thousandths of a millimeter).

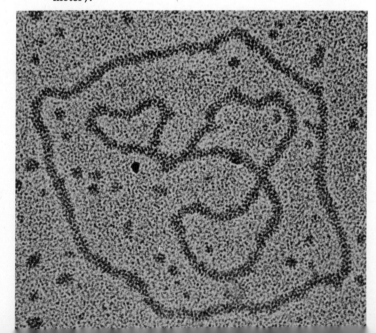

viruses of similar types cause cancer in animals. A recent report stated that the synthetic RNA protected mice and rabbits against *Herpes simplex* infection and inhibited growth of the virus in a culture of human cells.

Antibiotics, it should be mentioned, are not chemical drugs. They are cultures of living microorganisms. So we see that Pauling's prediction of molecular medicine is coming true. In other words, the fact that we can create life may in the long run prove to be of less importance than the application of the technique to the protection or improvement of human life.

7

Controlled Evolution

"For the first time in all time a living creature understands its origin and can undertake to design its future."

"The safest course would be to lock all of you up."

These two statements were made at recent scientific meetings. The first was made by Robert L. Sinsheimer, Professor of Biophysics at the California Institute of Technology, and the second by David Daube, Professor of Law at Oxford University. The statements summarize, on the one hand, the realization of the almost god-like power in man's hands and the optimism that something good can come of it, and, on the other, the knowledge that, as with nuclear power, it can be turned to evil as well as good.

In both cases, it is the enormity of what can be done that is so frightening. The awesome power and destructive ability of the atomic bomb is well known. But consider, an accidental change in a single gene—a bit of material perhaps one-millionth of an inch long—can cause a fly that normally has two wings to have four, or cause clubfeet in a man.

In Chapter 4, when we talked of making changes in genes, we were referring to the bringing of defective genes back to normal. In this chapter we are concerned with the possibilities of making deliberate changes in genes, changes that, hopefully, will result in "improvements" in the human being.

Dr. Krafft Ehricke, scientist and author, has written, "The development of the mammal, the most versatile and perfect land animal, was a brilliant biotechnical achievement. Divorcing the body from the ground, by means of legs, freed the body from slavishly following the temperature cycle of the soil. . . . Now it was no longer necessary to lay eggs and depend on the sun and hatching . . . life became independent of climatic conditions. The conquest of the land could be completed."

Man, of course, has come a long step beyond the other mammals. He has a brain some three times the size of his nearest relatives, the great apes. His feet are far better adapted for running and upright walking; thus his hands have been freed to develop into the highly dextrous instruments they now are.

He has added the creation and use of complex tools. And he has developed language and symbol manipulation that enable him not only to create more complex ideas and things, but to learn what someone far away has done and created, and so to be able to build upon that information.

We face, however, an important question: Has the physical evolution of man come to an end? Professor Theodosius Dobzhansky of Rockefeller University points out, for example, that "For at least 10,000 and perhaps for 1,000,000 years man has been adapting his environments to his genes more often than his genes to his enviroment." Thus if we were to enter another Ice Age, we would be far more likely to put on fur coats and build warmer houses than we would to grow fur.

The reader who knows something about evolution may well take objection to that last phrase: "than we would [be likely] to grow fur." The phrase implies that living things have the ability to grow or evolve new adaptations at will. In the normal situation, of course, this is not so. Normally, the potential ability of the genes to mutate in this direction are there, and natural selection takes care of the rest.

But man is not a normal animal, and we are talking of the future, not the past. And so the deliberate changing of his genes to grow a fur coat is a distinct possibility.

Before we go into how this might be done, let us consider a number of other possibilities. Some are humorous; some are serious; all are at least conceivable.

Some Proposed Changes in Man

Consider first our all-purpose mouth, which is used for eating, talking, whistling, drinking, breathing, chewing, biting, smiling, grimacing, moistening envelope flaps, and even, on occasion, for helping the hands, as in moistening thread for threading needles or carrying something while searching for a key. "Imagine," writes Professor R. C. W. Ettinger, "the incalculable benefit in teen-age happiness alone, if one could eat, chew gum, and talk on the telephone, all at the same time—without the danger of strangling."

Or how about our mode of person-to-person communication? Speech has served man well for thousands of years, but is it necessarily the best way? At noisy gatherings or dances, for instance, one is never quite sure he heard what his partner was saying. It may also be that man's ever-increasing complexity of thought and expression requires some other, more flexible technique. Perhaps a small screen that could flash rapidly changing forms and colors might be able to get across more, and more subtle forms of, information. Perhaps, as with television, this could supplement the purely verbal form of communication.

Other possibilities of communications are touch and various

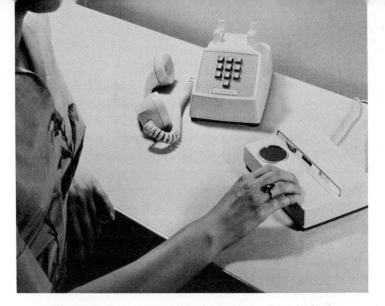

This Code-Com set for the deaf shows that methods other than the spoken word are possible for person-to-person communication. The set, connected to a conventional telephone, allows a deaf person to "see" speech in coded flashes of light or "feel" them in vibrations of a finger pad. Light flashes come from black rectangle at rear, vibrations from circular pad at left. The sending key, used like a telegraph key, is at right. This could be one step along the way toward a new, expanded method of person-to-person communication.

forms of chemical methods (as practiced by many animal species).

And how about our senses? Delicate and flexible though they are, are they the ultimate? Butterflies have their taste sense in their feet—useful because they walk on their food. It seems that young children especially would be delighted to have such a sense. Perhaps there are other adjustments that could be made in our senses. A few years ago there was a flurry of excitement when it was thought that some people had been found who had a visual or color sense in their fingertips. This turned out to be either a hoax or a highly developed sense of skin temperature (dark colors would be warmer than light ones). Assuming it could be developed, such a sense might be useful.

Bees' eyes are said to be sensitive both to ultraviolet light and to polarized light. The latter ability might help man navigate when lost and without a compass or other means of direction-finding. Perhaps a built-in magnetic sense could do the same. And how about a sonar or infrared sense (as are possessed by bats and snakes, respectively) for finding our way about in the dark? Also certain species of fish create an electric field around them and can thus detect when a strange object moves within range of the field by its distortion. This would be very useful for some forms of self-defense or perhaps even in sports.

Speaking of sports, probably every athlete has longed at some time for longer arms. Granted this might be a little awkward as a permanent change; but how about an extendible arm, useful in a number of sports, including tennis, boxing, baseball, football, and basketball.

Another popular sport is scuba diving. Imagine how much more fun this would be if we could breathe underwater, without special equipment. Fish do it, why can't we? As a matter of fact, humans go through a stage before birth when they do have gills like fish. (The gills are not functional, however.) Such a change would be useful for other reasons than that of sport. More and more, we will be turning to the oceans for natural resources, food, exploration, and, perhaps, even living space. All of this would be far more convenient if we could breathe underwater.

Man is tampering so much with his environment that it may one day be necessary to develop resistance to radioactivity, to heat or cold, to chemicals in our water and air, or who knows to what else.

For example, the vast quantities of energy he uses require the burning of enormous quantities of fuel; one result is an increase of carbon dioxide in the atmosphere along with a decrease in oxygen. The decrease in oxygen could have obviously disastrous effects, since we depend directly upon it. "Already," says Professor Firsoff, "remarkable changes have been observed in the composition of proteins and enzymes as the oxygen content of the air decreases, the plants giving off unusual gases, such as carbon monoxide and hydrogen." Thus we may have to "learn" to breathe some other mixture of gases. While other types of life are known to exist on earth that do not require oxygen, such as certain types of bacteria, they are all (so far) lower forms of life.

Two possible, and contradictory, results have been forecast as a result of the increasing content of carbon dioxide and other pollutants in the atmosphere. Some scientists suggest that the earth will get colder as the "thickening" atmosphere (caused by increasing amounts of dust in the air) blocks out some of the sun's rays. On the opposite side are those who suggest that higher quantities of carbon dioxide would make the earth warmer. Even now we are subject to a "greenhouse effect" in which the atmosphere, due largely to the carbon dioxide and water vapor in it, allows a large part of the sun's rays to pour down on the earth, but absorbs much of the longer-wave infrared radiation that is sent back out by the earth. This infrared radiation, which is what we usually feel as heat, is then radiated both upward and downward. An increase in the effect would therefore tend to heat up the earth.

If the earth cools, we may want to grow fur coats after all. Or, if we stick with clothes, then perhaps we might develop a separate set of orifices for exhalation of used air. If this air, which has been warmed by circulating through the lungs, were emitted from an orifice near the waist (in a manner similar to the blowholes of the whales and dolphins), then the heat contained therein would not be immediately lost to the atmosphere.

On the other hand, if the earth heats up we may have to

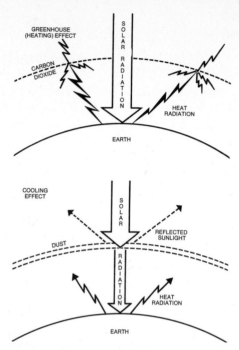

Heating vs. cooling effects in the atmosphere.

change our proportions altogether: long, pipe-stem legs and arms, for instance, are effective heat radiators. Should things really get bad, it may be necessary to change our body chemistry as well. After all, water boils at only a little more than twice our normal body temperature. It may therefore be necessary to replace our carbon-centered system with silicon, which is more heat-resistant. Should this actually be possible (and I don't say it is or isn't), and should the population explosion continue unabated for a long enough period, then it might also be useful for many to find homes deep in the earth's hot interior.

With vast numbers of people on earth, obtaining enough food would obviously also become a problem. Again, there are several possibilities. Great numbers of plants, such as woody plants containing cellulose, are found inedible by humans. Perhaps we could change our digestive systems in such a way that we could utilize such plants, as cows do, by the use of special bacteria in a specially adapted digestive system. We might even go a step further. Animals, in general, cannot build carbon dioxide and water directly into living material as plants can. Perhaps man can, if necessary, learn to perform this little trick. It might of course mean the need for great green ears or some other means of trapping large quantities of sunlight, but then why worry about details now? Another way around the food problem is to reduce the size of our species. This would save space as well.

Professor James Bonner once told Lawrence Lessing, the science writer, "I have tried to think about what further organs I would like to have, and I have decided that I would like to have four hands, since there is so much for biologists to do.

"Recently," he continued, "as I was trying to light my pipe in the laboratory, my colleague, Professor Huang, said to me, 'If you're going to smoke a pipe in the laboratory, you'll need five.'"

It might also be useful if the second set of hands had different-sized fingers. Thus we would have one size for heavy tasks, and another for delicate work.

Returning for a moment to the subject of our environment, we are faced with all kinds of pollution: air, water, land, thermal (heat), even noise pollution. The momentum of increasing pollution has been so great that it may actually be easier at some time in the future to adapt man to his changing environment than the reverse. It is no longer necessary for man to be ever on the alert against attack by other animals, as it once was; hence some form of "ear-lids" to screen out unwanted noise might one day be desirable or even necessary. The porpoise has them, although the major purpose for his is apparently to protect his delicate eardrums when he dives deeply.

Mutations—changes in gene structure that lie at the heart

of whatever changes have taken place in the history of life—are usually caused by something. This could be an accidental "hit" by radiation from the earth, the atmosphere, or from outer space in the form of high-speed nuclear particles or electromagnetic radiation (such as X-rays). Ultraviolet radiation is known to be mutagenic (mutation-inducing), as are a number of chemicals. And, as you know, we live in a world that is being drowned in a sea of chemicals. James F. Crow, a medical geneticist, has urged that more attention be given to possible chemical mutagens. "In our complex chemical society," he says, "it is quite possible that some widely used compounds are highly mutagenic."

It seems likely that the future will see an even greater danger of unwanted mutation. Perhaps biologists will have to make a major change in man's genes to make them more stable and less susceptible to accidental mutation!

You may have noticed that we have not yet mentioned the brain, that organ which, more than any other, distinguishes man from beast. Although we will have more to say about the brain later, here are a few small suggestions: First and most obvious is an increase in size. This, however, might make trouble in the birth process, as it has in the history of man's evolution. As the size of the brain increased, so did that of the skull. In order for it still to be possible for the head to pass through the birth opening, the infant's skull is formed of soft plates that do not solidify into a solid until much later in life. How much further this could be carried is questionable. Perhaps test-tube births are the answer.

Another approach is to increase the temperature of the brain, which may or may not require increasing the entire body temperature. As we mentioned earlier, higher temperatures increase the speed of chemical activity. It seems somehow logical that this would aid in the operation of the brain. This may be a coincidence, but Alfred Russel Wallace, who came up with the idea of evolution at the same time as Darwin, is said to have had his brainstorm while laid up with some sort of fever!

And how about building a switch onto the connection between the two halves of the brain so that, if we wish, we can concentrate on two intellectual tasks at the same time?* This presupposes that the tasks are not so complicated as to require our full attention and brain capacity, as most of them are not.

Making the Changes

Now that we have discussed some of the things that might be done, the question is, "How?" One approach, that of genetic engineering, or molecular surgery, has already been discussed. We have seen that the process certainly seems possible, though we are nowhere near being able to carry it out.

* The brain obviously is performing many *physical* tasks in the control of the body all the time.

The late Dr. Herman J. Muller received the Nobel Prize in 1946 for his discovery that X-rays can cause mutations. Dr. Muller was also a strong believer in eugenics and genetic engineering.

There is another way that is closer to reality, though just how close and how practicable it is, is a matter of controversy. The method is called *eugenics*, a combination of the Greek *eu*, which means good or advantageous, and *gene*. The objective of eugenics is to improve the human race. The British scientist Francis Galton (a cousin of Charles Darwin) proposed a eugenics program just a century ago. The basic idea was to replace natural selection with artificial selection. The idea, however, was not new, at least as far as plants and animals are concerned. Man has been artificially breeding plants and animals for thousands of years. That is how he

Triticale, the first man-made grain, is a cross between durum wheat and rye. It has a long head, is high in protein, resists drought, and yields well, but at present has poor milling qualities.

has domesticated the dog, cat, cow, and many other creatures. That is how racing horses and purebred, or pedigreed, dogs are created. A particular trait, such as long legs in a horse or a long body in a dog, is singled out and the animal is bred for it. Only those animals with that trait are allowed to mate and produce offspring. If this is continued long enough, a "purebred" variety of the species is created. The speed of the racing horse or the long body of the Dachshund is the result. Perhaps we could breed a race of extremely clever apes to take over many of the boring, repetitive jobs that must now be done by people.

Another approach is to cross two animals or plants in an attempt to combine certain desirable characteristics. Plant biologists (botanists), for example, have developed strains of wheat that combine the good productivity of one type with the hardiness and resistance to disease of another, thus providing vast improvements in yield. In some cases, countries that have been short of food for centuries have been turned in this way into food exporters.

Eugenicists would like to apply similar methods in the reproduction of man. And who can argue against the picture of a future race of long-lived, honorable, healthy, generous, handsome, courageous mental giants? One need only think back to the first mammals to realize how far man has come. The theologian P. Teilhard de Chardin has written that "Man is the ascending arrow of the great biological synthesis. Man is the last-born, the keenest, the most complex, the most subtle of the successive layers of life."

But why assume we have reached the end of the line? What incredible heights may man yet reach?

The genetic counselors we mentioned earlier are, in a sense, eugenicists. But they are performing what might be called negative eugenics; by counseling two people who have the same undesirable gene not to marry or not to have chil-

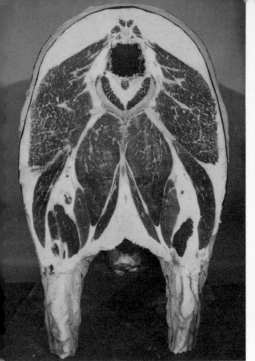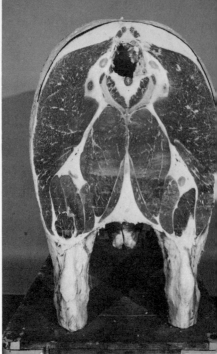

Two hind sections of beef. See how selective breeding has improved the ratio of meat to fat in the steer on the right.

dren, they are in effect attempting to eliminate that gene from the human species.

The other side of the coin would of course be positive eugenics, which is to say, increasing the frequency of superior genes. But here is where we run into trouble, in several ways.

A Superior Breed?

When we breed roses, our objective is simple enough: We want large size, or perhaps a different color, or some such characteristic. When we breed sheep, the variety with the thickest wool is said to be superior.

But what do we really mean by a superior person? Surely Einstein was one of the great geniuses of our era; but he was hardly the picture of a Greek god. Suppose then he had mated with Miss Universe. Would the result be the brains of Einstein and a strong, beautiful body? Not necessarily. It could just as easily have been the rather short, soft body of Einstein and the brains of Miss Universe. (No offense intended.)

If everyone could be given a superb body, filled with great physical energy and "tuned" just right, is it not possible that many of those who might otherwise have spent their early years poring over books would now be out on the playing fields because they simply couldn't sit still? Is it not possible that we would in effect lose some of our finest scholars? One might say that there is plenty of time for them to get their learning and early development done later on. But it has been shown that many scientists, particularly mathematicians and physicists, do their best and most creative work in their teens and early twenties.

The idea of a god-like race of geniuses may be a pure fictional concept. Often genius is possessed by a selfish person.* To a certain extent this may even be necessary. It may also be the way a person can overcome a lesser endowment. There are people with apparently great natural ability who never accomplish anything of note, while others with seemingly less natural ability go on to great heights, often at the expense of their personal lives and those of their loved ones. What do you "breed" for? Haldane has remarked that to create a race of angels we would need mutations for both the wings and the moral excellence.

We can even carry this further. Beethoven, acknowledged to be one of the greatest composers of all time, turned to composing because a growing deafness barred a promising career as a pianist. The Greek poet Homer was blind, and

---

* Lev Landau, when asked if he had ever spoken with Einstein, answered, "Yes, but little. It was difficult to speak with him since I did not interest him. Nobody interested him. He was too preoccuupied with himself."

the Russian writer Dostoevsky had epilepsy. At this point we simply do not know whether this was coincidence, or if there is some connection between the problem and the accomplishment, as for instance, a determined attempt to overcome a disability.

In some cases there might even be a physical connection. As Garrett Hardin, a Professor of Biology, says, "It is more than merely conceivable that a person with 'schizophrenic genes' may not be an overt schizophrenic,* but rather may become president of a corporation, a college professor, or a mathematician." In other words, even so-called defective genes may confer an advantage of which we are not yet aware, just as the crimped red blood cells of those suffering from sickle cell anemia have a natural immunity against malaria. "With increasing knowledge," Hardin continues, "I think we will discover many dilemmas of this sort."

It has even been shown that a gene may have a favorable effect in one combination, and an unfavorable effect in another.

The point is that, so far at least, no such thing as a superior gene has ever been identified in man. Not only that, but those qualities we most admire—intelligence, strength, health, strength of character, and so on—are not dependent on single genes. Thus breeding for (or genetically engineering) an improvement in one area may very well result in a deterioration in another. The British biologist P. B. Medawar suspects that "some element of tameness or docility of domesticated animals (e.g., sheep and cattle) is the product of selection for frank mental deficiency; and" he continues, "I wonder how tame rats compare in intelligence with wild rats."

Perhaps it would be wisest not to make any moves in the direction of genetic engineering until we have done all

---

* Schizophrenia is a severe mental and emotional sickness, often characterized by the patient's loss of contact with his surroundings and disintegration of personality.

we can in the area of "cultural" engineering. That is to say, our valuation of desirable and undesirable traits (such as low mental ability) are all mixed up with social, cultural, and environmental problems. We are still not sure how much of a person's mental ability is hereditary and how much environmental (and/or which parts).

Recently, Dr. Albert Szent-Györgyi, Nobel Prize winner in medicine, was asked whether he could improve on nature. His answer was:

> The main result of my research, stretching over more than five decades, is a deep admiration for the harmony and perfection of nature. . . . Living systems have a built-in mechanism for improving themselves which we understand but partly. It had all the time, millions or billions of years, to do its work. It seems difficult to add to it.

The well-known biologist Dr. René Dubos went even further: "Any attempt to alter the human body," he wrote, "is a biological, intellectual and ethical monstrosity."[*]

It may even be that we will not be able to breed ourselves free of *un*desirable genes—even assuming everyone conferred with and cooperated with genetic counselors. For one thing, most of the genes that are now felt to be undesirable are recessive. In such cases non-reproduction by the affected persons would work very slowly. It is said that it would take two thousand years to wipe out something like albinism. And even then, mutations would still undoubtedly cause defects to reappear occasionally.

Perhaps the approach that will one day be taken will be a combination of eugenic breeding wherever possible, with the application of genetic engineering when necessary.

Or it may just be that further development of man's technology—and the combination of man and machine—may make much of this unnecessary.

[*] "Man Revised," *The Sciences,* December 1969, p. 26.

8

Man and Machine

İt is probably not too far from the truth to say that many of man's machines are simply extensions of himself. His cars and aircraft are extensions of his feet, while derricks and pneumatic drills are extensions of his hands. Some of his machines are not so much physical extension as functional ones. Thus washing machines take over the function of hand-washing and vacuum cleaners of rug-beating.

In almost every case, the machine is built to perform a single specialized job. On the other hand, man's strength is his versatility—the fact that he can do an extraordinarily large number of things at least passably well. Clearly, the ultimate machine would be one that could do many of these things even better than man. The science fiction fan will think immediately of the android. This is a full-sized man- or woman-like creature that is constructed artificially. It is a machine, since it is built in a factory or workshop; and, as usually conceived, its "insides" consist of springs, motors, wheels, and computers. Although normally it will have some superhuman characteristics, such as great strength or endurance or sensory ability (stories about superpeople and supermachines form an important part of science fiction), it can nevertheless be made in such a way that from the outside no one can tell that it is not human.

Sometimes humans even fall in love with them. I once saw a television play in which a man working on a distant planet falls in love with a girl, only to find out that she is an android. Toward the end of the play a spaceship arrives to take him back to Earth, but he wants to bring his "girl" back with him. Unfortunately, there is no room for her. The man refuses to go, whereupon his "rescuer," impatient to get going, shoots the girl in cold blood. But of course there is no blood, only springs and wheels that spurt out of the hole blasted in her stomach. Her lover looks at her for a long while and then, sadly, boards the spaceship. Fade-out.

Such a realistic android is pretty far out and won't be seen—I don't think—in my time. Nevertheless, androids are no longer the exclusive property of the science fiction writer; scientists are thinking about them more and more; and a few tentative steps have already been made along the way.

Perhaps it would be well, before we talk about these steps, to consider the question, "Why bother with androids?" We have more than enough people already. And there is certainly no problem in making new ones. Also, machines can be made to handle almost any particular job. Usually the reason for considering an android is that the job to be done is not highly specialized, but is difficult, dangerous, or otherwise not fit for a human. Another reason is that androids of various sorts and levels of complexity may help us understand ourselves better. Engineers often construct models before building the final product, while scientists will try to build a physical model, if possible, of a theoretical idea.

From a physical or "action" point of view, the significant thing about the android is that man need not control or pre-program his every move. The engineer would say that man is not part of the control loop. In a science fiction story, the android's instructions might be simply, "Jlorb has been captured by the Flimbiks; bring him back." This is a very specific job; but the android is usually given all the latitude in the universe to carry out the mission.

When the androids are built—and I can see no reason to doubt that they will be—some interesting questions will arise. If they are truly indistinguishable from man, and perhaps even smarter (more about this later), what kind of laws will be required to handle the situation?

Will an android be a citizen of the country in which it was "born," entitled to all rights and privileges? Will it be "owned" by its creators (that one man could build it is very unlikely), as a horse is owned by its master? Could it be bought and sold, like a dog? Will there be an American Society for the Prevention of Cruelty to Androids?

Will it have feelings and consciousness, as well as intelligence? There seems to be a growing feeling that if all the physical equipment is there—enough neurons, interconnections, senses—then other so-called human attributes such as emotions, drive, and will to survive, will also exist.

And how about parent-child relationships? We have seen that "test-tube babies" are a definite possibility. Indeed, a child may not even need two parents in the future, but may be derived from a skin cell or other cell of a single "parent."

Surely one who builds a true biological android from scratch can be as much a parent as he, or she, who donates a cell or two.

But of course there are specific differences between the "natural" person and the android. When you turn off a machine at night, it is truly off. Its fuel requirements go down to zero. But when a man goes to sleep at night, he still uses something like one-third as much fuel (energy) as when he is awake and doing light work. For example, every second of your life, some 3 million red blood cells die and must be replaced. (Even if a machine requires some energy for purposes of air conditioning or whatever, this will be small compared to its normal needs.)

Perhaps then this will be the way to distinguish between man and machine, i.e., see what its fuel requirements are when "turned off."

Another difference is that a living thing is made of the same kind of material it consumes, while an engine is made of metal. Imagine an engine made of wood or coal.

If an android is manufactured, the implication is that it is built to its final size, so that it starts out as an adult, at least physically. Most likely it will have to be programmed, trained, or whatever. This will correspond to its mental childhood. But from what we saw in the last chapter, it might be possible to program it in a very short time, by means of injections, pills, or perhaps electricity. (The analogy has been made of the phonograph record that contains an hour or more of information but takes less than a second to press.)

Indeed, we can carry the confusion even further. A human being is a fearfully complex piece of equipment. Building one (or a reasonably complete copy) would clearly be far more time-consuming and difficult than constructing the most complicated piece of equipment that has ever been built— whatever it might be. Perhaps, if androids are built, they will be made the same way that "real" people are. That is to say, they will start as a single cell, but one that has been artificially put together, and then grown. Or perhaps "cultured" would be a better word. Thus a shipment of "humans" to a distant planet could be easily transported in a thimble-sized container. If necessary or desirable, the rate of growth can probably be speeded up considerably, even ten or twenty times the norm. Thus we could have a 20-year-old in one or two years. Its metabolic machinery can, perhaps, be designed to be more efficient and to operate on special fuels (food?) so that there is no waste. It can be designed to be immune to disease. Many normal living molecules are "right-handed."

115

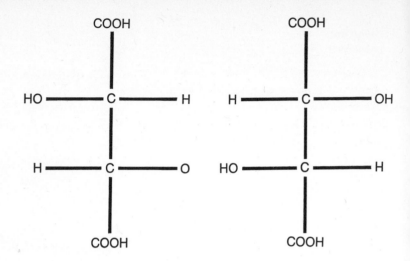

LEFT HANDED   RIGHT HANDED

Racemic tartaric acid, found in inanimate (non-living) matter, is an equal mixture of "left-handed" and "right-handed" molecules. Only the "right-handed" form, however, is found in living things.

Perhaps if its atoms are reversed, disease-bearing organisms will not be interested in it. The possibilities are endless.

We are of course a long way away from the advent of the android, at least partially because there is not that much need for it, at least not in the sense in which it is found in science fiction. Man is both a mental and a physical being. Virtually all the mental jobs the android might tackle are handled very nicely by computer (more about this in the next chapter), while the vast majority of the physical jobs can be handled in other ways. In most cases, more specialized types of equipment can be built far more cheaply, especially if man is kept in the control loop.

Manipulators

Probably the best example of this type of equipment is found in nuclear energy facilities, where it is used to handle radioactive materials. It is part of a broad class of devices called manipulators, master-slaves, or sometimes teleoperators (*tele* means distance or far in Greek). As with androids, the significant thing about manipulators is that they are general-purpose machines—as opposed, for example, to a similar device on an automated factory line that may be even more complicated but which does the same thing all the time.

A mechanical "hand," which can repeat many of the motions of a normal hand, is directed by the operator. He, in turn, is guided by information, usually visual, that enables him to carry out the process. He may be able to see directly through a radiation-proof shield, or the information may have to be brought to him via a periscope arrangement, or perhaps through television, depending on the application. An unmanned undersea explorer clearly would require television.

Such devices may also be used for applications requiring an amplification of strength—a powerful "arm" and "hand" for heavy-duty jobs requiring greater dexterity than a crane or derrick.

The more sophisticated manipulators not only provide a visual picture of what is going on, but also provide what is called force feedback, a feeling in the gripping apparatus for how much pressure is actually being applied. In the through-the-wall, mechanical type, the operator provides the power, though there are some losses through friction and the weight of the equipment. In remote applications, such as undersea or in space, the operator is providing only the instructions to the machine; the driving force is external—electric motors or compressed air, for example—and the operator would have no idea of how much pressure he is applying. Thus force sensors are built into the digits or "fingers" of the manipulator, and this information is sent back to the handling controls. The difference is a little bit like what happened in the early forms of automobile power-steering. The steering wheel

117

worked so easily that the driver lost "the feel of the road" and tended to oversteer because the wheel offered no resistance. Now most power-steering systems reflect some of the resistance to turning back into the steering wheel. We shall see later that this is exactly what happens, although in a much more sensitive and complex form, in our own limbs.

While industry and research have made good use of manual

Experimental four-legged walking device developed for the Army for use in rough terrain is controlled by the actions of its operator. The front legs mimic the operator's arm motions; the rear legs mimic his leg motions.

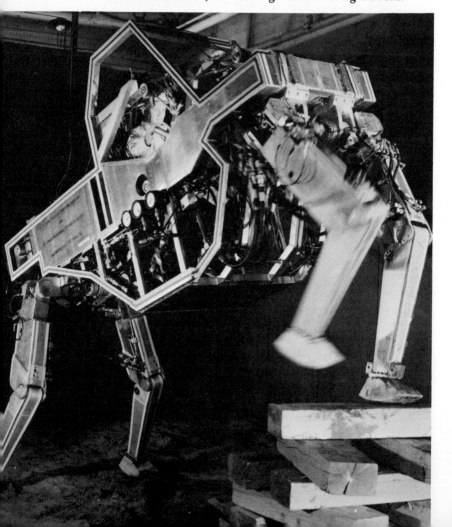

Experimental unpowered exoskeleton. A powered version might make it possible for a man's strength to be magnified ten or more times.

manipulators, the armed forces, particularly the army, have begun to wonder whether something similar might not be done for the feet. Aside from firing power, the most important characteristic of a good unit is mobility. Jeeps can go almost anywhere. But that word "almost" can sometimes spell trouble. Thus work has been going on in developing "pedipulators"—two- or four-legged, machine-aided walking devices that will indeed be able to go anywhere. See illustration.

The ultimate outcome will probably be a more intimate

association of man and machine. One possibility, shown here, is a mechanical frame (sometimes called an exoskeleton) that can be strapped onto a man. It will not only mimic his every motion, but will magnify his strength. This "man-amplifier" might, for example, be used for lifting 1,000-pound crates in cramped quarters. Perhaps someday the awkward-looking skeleton will be replaced by a comfortable suit comparable to the parachutist's jump suit, or the astronaut's space suit. Various names, such as Optiman (optimum man), and Hardiman, have been given to the result.

Different Kinds of Androids

And beyond that, the androids again. Not only will androids be useful in ways other than bringing back Jlorb, but they will be made on many levels. Highly realistic dummies are already used, for instance, in crash tests of cars to see whether a new safety device does any good. Clearly it would be dangerous to put any man, no matter how well protected, in such a situation. Sensors placed in strategic positions on the dummy provide needed information at the time of impact, while examination afterward shows probable extent of damage to a real human.

Even more realistic is a model patient at the University of Southern California School of Medicine. The word *model* can be taken two ways. It is a model in that medical students can experiment with the device as much as they please without its ever complaining to the administration. And it is a model in that it is an imitation of a human patient. And a very good one it is, too. It breathes, and has a heartbeat and pulse; its pupils can dilate and contract; it can stick out its tongue, wrinkle its eyebrows, cough, twitch, change color from a healthy pink to an unhealthy gray; and it can even have a heart attack.

A major function of the model is to give the students

The "Beast" finds its own way down a corridor and "explores" at leisure. When its batteries run down the device will seek a wall outlet and recharge itself to the proper level. It finds the outlet and avoids danger (such as walls and stairs) by means of sensitive microswitch sensors, which simulate our sense of touch.

practice in inserting a tube down its throat, a tricky procedure that is best not practiced on living patients. Other, non-medical, characteristics, such as the ability to walk, could have been built into the model. But they would add greatly to its cost and would have added nothing to its purpose.

Such a device—and regardless of how realistic it is, it is no more than that—can be called a *physical* analogue or model of a living thing, in this case, man.

On the other side of the coin are the mental/emotional characteristics of living things. Experimentation along these lines is taking place as well, at least partly as a way of helping us understand these characteristics in living things. An important characteristic of living things is a desire to stay alive. Well, consider the device shown here. Nicknamed "the Beast," it was constructed by a group at Johns Hopkins Applied Physics Laboratory. It will move toward light, as many animals do, and will turn and take another direction when it bumps into an obstacle. It will move about at a leisurely pace, but only until its batteries start to run down. At that point its pace speeds up and it automatically begins to seek out a wall outlet to recharge its batteries. When it accomplishes this, it resumes its leisurely "explorations."

At M.I.T., a machine has been built that can catch a ball thrown at it; another can utilize a randomly placed supply of various size blocks and build a tower from them just as a child would.

What is significant about these devices is that they mimic some of the activities of living things, but are neither controlled by man nor pre-programmed.

Nevertheless, few would confuse these with living things. In the world of the future this distinction may be more difficult to make. For many of the "machines" may be grown biologically! A number of ideas have already been put forth for machines that grow, reproduce, and repair themselves. R. R. Landers, author of an interesting book called *Man's Place in the Dybosphere*, even wonders whether stronger machines might not overpower weaker ones if they need spare parts that are unavailable in any other way.

Prosthetics

You needn't fear that you will be replaced by an android in the near future. Although scientists have been able to provide electronic larynxes and pacemakers that stabilize heartbeat in those who need them, they have yet to provide an amputee with even a good artificial arm and hand. By good, I mean one that is both realistic looking and functional.

The branch of medicine that is concerned with the addition of an artificial part to the body is called *prosthetics*. We shall also discuss the possibilities of artificially giving a paralyzed

or weakened limb strength and dexterity. This field is called
orthotics.

As with manipulators, there are two basic approaches to
control of the limb in question. The less common one is to
pre-program a sequence of movement that add up to some
function such as feeding oneself, turning the pages of a book,
and so on. This is equivalent to setting the temperature and
wash time on an automatic washer, then pushing the button
to get it started. For one who is paralyzed, a particular motion
of an eye, eyebrow, or even tongue could be enough to start
the program. An artificial limb is used for an amputee, while
one whose limb is paralyzed is supplied with a powered
frame or splint-like arrangement.

This approach is far more difficult than it may seem, for it
requires some sort of computer and a complete program of
instructions for each function, as well as energy (electrical,

**Over 9,000 people who have lost their voices through
paralysis or surgery have been helped to speak again
with the help of an artificial larynx.**

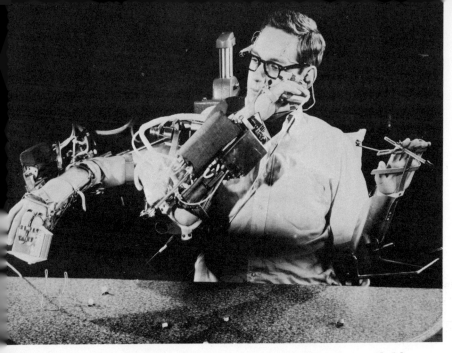

Programmed control of a paralyzed arm is provided by
the Case Research Arm Aid. At left, patient is picking
up an electric razor and, at center, shaving.

hydraulic, or pneumatic) to provide the power. Further, even
the simplest repetitive activity, such as turning the pages of a
book, is really a highly complex series of motions, and requires
a delicate interplay of instructions, muscular actions, and
visual and tactile cues to be sure that the page is turned and
not ripped out of the book. This approach is still very much
in the experimental stage.

The more common approach is to somehow allow the wearer
to directly control each of the motions, as the operator does
with manipulators. The problem, of course, is that the wearer
does not have a normal hand, with its many possible motions,
to use for directing the apparatus. The most important single
activity of the hand is that of grasping something between
thumb and finger(s). In most artificial hands or hooks the
grasping action is a simple, pliers-type motion that is controlled by some muscular activity, such as shrugging a shoul-

der. Although the wearers become remarkably dexterous, they are still obviously very limited in their range of activities.

Oddly enough, it is not the missing muscle power that is the big problem. Although the perfect power source has certainly not yet been found, satisfactory substitutes have been and are being developed. Use can be made of other muscles in the body, nuclear- or battery-powered electricity, and compressed air from a small portable tank. Small power plants fed by electricity and/or chemicals from the body are also being experimented with.

The major problem is providing sufficient, and sufficiently accurate, information at the right time, and in the right sequence, to make a complex set of motions not only possible but convenient. Undoubtedly the most intriguing lead is the fact that when a limb is severed, the remaining muscles do not die or disappear, though they may weaken and shrivel if not used. It has been found that a small electrical signal is generated in the muscle when the amputee thinks about moving the limb that that muscle used to control. (Before you lift your arm, you must—unknowingly perhaps—command certain mus-

First human implant of a radioisotope-powered pacemaker was performed on a 50-year-old French woman in 1970. Material used to power the device is Plutonium 238.

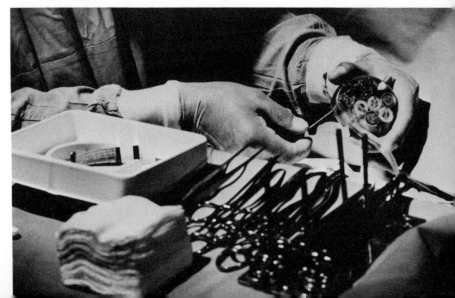

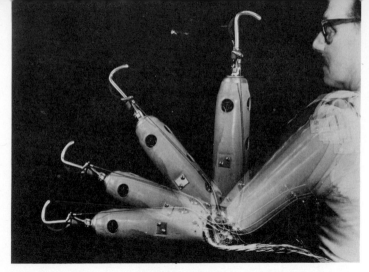

The "Boston Arm" utilizes electromyographic signals
generated in the muscles of the wearer.

cles in your arm to contract.) If an electrode is buried in one
of these muscles, it will pick up the electric signal that is
generated, and, as in a teleoperator, this can be used as a
control signal. These signals are called *myoelectric* (*myo* is
a Greek combining-form meaning muscle) or *electromyographic* (EMG). It has been found possible to electronically
blend EMG signals from various muscles in the body and in
this way to provide amputees with almost natural control over
their artificial limbs.

In their book *Teleoperators and Human Augmentation*, E.
G. Johnson and W. R. Corliss suggest:

> As myoelectric control becomes better understood it may
> supplement or replace hand-and foot-operated controls in
> other teleoperators with a normal, electrode-festooned opera-
> tor at the helm. This would be just a step short of tele-
> operator thought control.

But what is thought? You may be surprised to find out that
we really don't know, and that research into the question
has recently become as much a biochemical as a psychological
or philosophical endeavor.

126

9

Brain and Mind

As PROFOUND AS are the implications of possible physical changes and additions to the human being, they pale by comparison with what the future may hold in store for us with respect to advancements in the field of the intellect.

For it is our mental capacity, not our physical prowess or even appearance, that really distinguishes us from our animal cousins. Think of how much further removed we are from our nearest relatives, the apes, in mental capacity than in appearance. And think of the difference our mental capacity makes in the way we live.

Think too of how different our descendants might be if the size of their brains were doubled. This might only require inducing the cells of the brain to double just once more. Or perhaps just increasing the thickness or area of the outer layer of the brain, the cerebral cortex, might do the trick.

It may not even be necessary to do that much. For, as we mentioned earlier, with understanding comes control. And we are coming closer to an understanding of the workings of the mind—consciousness, memory, and learning.

127

Suppose someone could learn twice as fast, remember twice as much, think twice as well (whatever that may mean). Such a person might be almost as different from us as we are from the apes. In spite of the many ingenious "superman" stories to be found in the annals of science fiction, we are no more able to understand and predict what such a being would be like than an ape can understand us. (Dog and cat lovers think their animals understand them; but this is a very limited use of the term. They "understand" when they are liked, or disliked, or feared, but not much more.)

But there are other possibilities implied in the word *control*. This could also be taken to mean the control of men's minds (usually by those with evil intentions). Thus there are two major areas of the mind that we will investigate in this chapter—the intellectual and the emotional.

Body and Brain

Not too long ago, including a discussion of the mind in a book on biology would have been considered ridiculous. A well-known biology textbook, dated 1963, does not even have an entry in its index for the word. And the brain is covered in just 4 pages—out of a total of 755. Yet, it is worth noting, although the weight of the brain is only about one-fiftieth that of the rest of the body, it requires some 20 to 25 per cent of the body's oxygen-rich blood supply.

In one experiment, a pituitary growth hormone was injected into the tails of pregnant rats. When the rat fetuses were examined their brains were found to be heavier than usual, demonstrating that the size of the brain can be affected by external causes.

Further, the mind has traditionally been thought of in a strictly non-physical way, as a sort of disembodied aspect of the brain. Yet already today, says Dr. David Krech of the

University of California, a class of drugs has been discovered that appears to speed up the learning and memory ability of experimental animals and older people. Although it is not yet clear whether these drugs will work on the average person, it is clear that biology can no longer afford to leave the mind to other scientists. Indeed, it has been found that anger, fear, aggression, pleasure, and a number of other emotions can be stimulated at will in experimental subjects by directing drugs or electricity at certain parts of the brain. Brain surgery has also been found to have an effect on behavior.

The artificial distinction that has traditionally been drawn between brain and mind, or between matter and mind, is disappearing. "In a certain sense," Professor T. Dobzhansky has written, "all else in the life sciences is only the background for an attempt to understand man and man's mind." Indeed, it has even been said that the body is nothing more than an inefficient vehicle for carrying the mind from one task to the next.

It is hard for today's youth, who perhaps hear too much about drugs, to realize that the association between drugs and mind is a very recent one—less than two decades—at least in our society. Even the field of psychiatry had been dominated for most of this century by "talk" therapy. This has changed enormously. Drugs are now commonly used to calm excited, aggressive patients and to perk up depressed ones.

But it is in the field of experimental biology that the most spectacular changes in mind research are taking place.

Electrical Stimulation of the Brain

Men have protected themselves against aggression from animals and other men in many interesting ways throughout history. But there is no doubt that a turning point was reached a few years ago when a biological researcher stood in a bullring armed with nothing but a cape and a radio transmitter.

At a given command the bull—an honest-to-goodness "brave bull"—was admitted into the ring. He looked around, focused on the red cape held by Dr. J. M. R. Delgado, Professor of Physiology at Yale University, and charged. The normal technique of the matador is to outmaneuver the bull by neatly sidestepping as he charges by. But Dr. Delgado held his ground. At the proper moment, he pushed a button on his radio transmitter. The bull stopped in mid-charge and turned aside.

The secret? Tiny electrodes that had been buried in the brain of the bull. Pushing the button resulted in a small electrical pulse in a certain portion of the bull's brain. Dr. Delgado points out that "the result seemed to be a combination of motor effect, forcing the bull to stop and turn to one side, plus behavioral inhibition of the aggressive drive. Upon repeated stimulation, the animal was rendered less dangerous

A new approach to bullfighting. Dr. J. M. R. Delgado faces a brave bull armed only with a radio transmitter.

The diameter of this monkey's pupil can be controlled as if it were the diaphragm of a camera lens. Constriction is caused by electrical stimulation of the section of the brain called the hypothalamus.

than usual, and for a period of several minutes would tolerate the presence of investigators in the ring without launching any attack." The technique is called Electrical Stimulation of the Brain, or ESB.

In other experiments, cats have been made to fear mice, a normally loving monkey mother ignored her child, a hungry monkey turned away a banana, and the pupil of one of another monkey's eyes was made to contract. In humans, a paralyzed arm was raised, a wide-awake person has been put to sleep, and a man who was subject to involuntary episodes of uncontrollable rage was to calm himself by pressing a button on his own small control console that he carried with him. In another case, an experimenter reported, "One could sit with one's hand on the knob and control the level of [the patient's] anxiety." Old and forgotten memories and tunes have been brought back to mind and repeated.

Immediately there springs to mind the possibility of totalitarian control of humans by means of implantation of electrodes into the minds of millions of people in order to keep them in line. Dr. Delgado does not see this as a likely event. He points out, for example, that "in each case the details of behavioral expression are related to an individual history which cannot be created by ESB."

In other words, there is an important distinction that must be made with respect to the button-pushing or dial-control of humans and that of garage doors and model planes. For there is a great difference between the amount of information involved in the control of a model plane and that of a human. In the latter case, Dr. Delgado points out, "button-pushing is only one small step in operating a complicated set of machinery." One might think of a space shot. You or I could push the final button that makes the 6-million-pound rocket take off, but a vast amount of preliminary work has taken place. Thus the early experiences of a living thing will have a great effect on how the stimulation operates. In one experiment a stimulated cat was very careful to direct his hostility in such a way as not to get himself into serious trouble. He was still using his experience.

Further, the implantation procedure is complex and time-consuming. (Dr. W. Ross Adey of the University of California believes, however, that some of these effects may be achievable without implantation. He is experimenting with the effects of eternal electric fields on the operation of the brain.)

In spite of the difficulties involved, these and other experiments have revealed the locations of certain functional parts of the brain. A large number of "motor" areas—for controlling the motion of hands, fingers, tongue, etc.—have been mapped. Speech and sleep centers have been found.

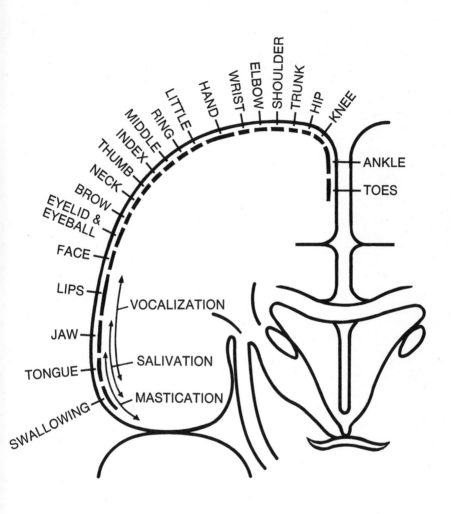

Localization of function in the cerebral cortex of a human brain. Control of particular muscular activities is shown in the cross section of the brain.

Perhaps the most extraordinary finding has been that of a so-called "pleasure center." One rat found the experience of being able to stimulate this pleasure center by pressing a lever so compelling that he did it to the exclusion of all else. Neither hunger nor thirst, nor even fatigue, stopped him. He kept pressing the lever, at the rate of some five thousand pushes per hour, until he simply keeled over from exhaustion.

To my mind the implications of this experiment are clear—and frightening. Mind control is usually thought of in terms of the bad dictator who makes his subjects do what he wants by force, or by forced use of drugs, hypnosis, electrical stimulation, or whatever. The implication is almost invariably that this is being done against the subject's will. But in *Brave New World* Aldous Huxley pointed out that "A really efficient totalitarian state would be one in which the all-powerful executive of political bosses and their army of managers control a population of slaves who do not have to be coerced, because they love their servitude."

In the novel, the working class is kept in line by a triple process of genetic manipulation before birth, psychological conditioning after birth, and a daily ration of "happy pills," which Huxley called soma. These pills also made the subject more suggestible—more amenable to orders and suggestions from the "top."

Already, as Huxley pointed out in a sequel, *Brave New World Revisited*, a "dictator could use tranquilizers to calm the excited, stimulants to arouse enthusiasm in the indifferent, [and] hallucinants to distract the attention of the wretched from their miseries."

How will he make his subjects take their pills? "In all probability," says Huxley, "it will be enough merely to make the pills available." A study done in 1968 showed that one American adult in four had taken a tranquilizer, sedative, or stimulant during the previous years. One in two had taken such a drug at least once. The wild-fire spread of drugs among today's youth attests to the truth of Huxley's statement.

Professor Z. M. Bacq, of the University of Liège in Belgium, is even more fearful of the future. He writes:

> Fresh, normal minds and bodies, devoid of 'complexes,' changing naturally from peaceful rest to agreeable stimulating work, will be rare birds in 1984, so rare that they will look abnormal in a drug-conditioned society. Instead of the wide spectrum of sharp and powerful individualities which have built mankind, we shall see a slow tide of eroded characters and [weakened] personalities.

Of course, drugs have been extremely useful in the field of mental health. Until about fifteen years ago, the number of mental cases in hospitals was rising steadily. With the introduction of the new mood-changing drugs, a downturn in admissions was noted for the first time in many years.

Science Digest reports that "anti-weather" pills are being tested on Polish bus drivers. Studies indicate that many people become depressed during bad weather, as for example during long periods of low atmospheric pressure. During this time accidents, suicides, heart failures, and other unpleasant occurrences all seem to increase. The pills come in two varieties: a stimulant to pick up those overcome by a feeling of lethargy (not caring about anything), and a different kind to calm those beset by nervousness.

One can imagine the complications that will arise when the use of pills, powders, and potions becomes even more widespread and common than it is now. Suppose James and Mary, normally a loving couple, wake up one morning on "opposite sides of the bed." That is to say, suppose he wakes up feeling low and Mary is feeling chipper and talkative. Mary of course wants James to perk up, while the last thing he wants is to hear a lot of bright chatter. So James slips a

135

powder into Mary's coffee that will quiet her down, while she slips a stimulant into his coffee. I leave the rest of the story to you.

Thus far the action of these types of drugs has been very general. That is, it has not been possible to cause a particular motor action (walk, sit down, etc.) or to stimulate rage in a normal subject by use of pills, as it has through ESB.

Chemical Stimulation of the Brain

A more direct kind of control has been achieved in a way that is closely allied with electrical stimulation of the brain. In what has come to be called Chemical Stimulation of the Brain, or CSB, chemical substances are dripped directly into specified portions of the brain through implanted hollow needles. As with ESB, there is no pain because brain tissue does not feel pain.

It is important to understand that these experiments did not arise with the idea of meddling with the lives of normal subjects. Rather, it had been guessed that what lay at the heart of certain forms of mental illness was an imbalance in one or more of the various chemical substances in the brain. This speculation started when drugs taken for a number of physical disorders produced effects that were disturbingly similar to those seen in certain mental disorders. The only way to find out which chemicals affect the human mental state was through controlled experiments.

Some of the results have been fascinating. One chemical injected into the brain of a rat who has had plenty of food and water will make him eat, nonetheless. A different chemical injected into the same place will make him drink. On the other hand, while stimulation of a certain area of the brain with a cholinergic chemical (one secreted by nerve fibers) causes sleep, cholinergic stimulation in a different area brings forth a wild rage.

The two techniques of ESB and CSB reflect the two major approaches to understanding the operation of the mind, namely, electrical and chemical. We talk about this in the next section.

The Mind

For many years the strange qualities of thought—evanescent as soap bubbles yet capable of rolling through generations of time—have led researchers to believe that there could be nothing physical involved, i.e., no physical change in the brain. To the great British neurologist Sir Charles Sherrington the mind was an "enchanted loom where millions of flashing shuttles weave a dissolving pattern, always a meaningful pattern though never an abiding one."

In other words, the closest we could come to an explanation of consciousness, thought, memory, and so on was that they were all some form of electrical activity. Thus a memory, for example, was an electrical circuit that had been built up and was reverberating somehow in the brain. Forgetting meant that the circuit, unused, perhaps, just died out.

Of all the mental activities of the brain the only one whose secrets we have been able to extract to even a limited degree has been that of memory. When rats were trained to accomplish a certain task, then given a shock to their brains immediately afterward, they lost all that training. Just as a light goes out, the memory was destroyed, supporting the idea of an electrical-circuit memory. But further experiments showed something additional. If the electric shock were given a quarter or a half hour later, the memory was only impaired, not wiped out altogether. And if the shock was delayed a day or two, the memory was not impaired at all.

Thus the evidence now points to a two- or even three-stage memory. The first is a primary phase lasting a half hour to perhaps an hour, in which some form of electrical loop or circuit maintains the information, such as a telephone number, in your memory just about long enough to dial it. Clearly it is just as well that you do not clutter up your memory with every telephone number you have ever looked up.

The "permanent" or stable storage of information appears to involve a structural change of some sort in your brain. No one is absolutely certain of just what this is, but it is believed to consist of changes in the protein or nucleic-acid molecules of the brain.

An intermediate stage lasts only a few hours and is probably also electrical.

In spite of the fact that our knowledge of what goes on in the brain is still very limited, some researchers are optimistic that much can be done to improve our minds. "Do you not feel with genius," wrote Sir George Thomson in 1955, "that it alone thinks naturally, while the rest of us block our thoughts perversely with irrelevancies?"

Professor David Krech is even more specific. He recently wrote in the *Saturday Review:*

> American educators now talk a great deal about the innovative hardware of education, about computer-assisted instruction, 8 mm. cartridge-loading projectors, microtransparencies, and other devices. In the not too distant future they may well be talking about enzyme-assisted instruction, protein memory consolidators, antibiotic memory repellers, and the chemistry of the brain.

Professor Henry Winthrop of the University of South Florida even foresees that "we shall learn how to transfer to ourselves the stored learning in other people's nervous systems and also to erase inaccuracies in the storage content of other people's learning as we now erase the unwanted contents of a magnetic tape."

138

The interaction of environment with the development of the brain is another area of considerable interest. In one experiment, test rats were taken out of their cages and fondled and played with for a specified time each day while a control group was left quite alone. Both groups were fed and otherwise treated similarly. The test group ended up larger and learned tasks faster than the control group.

It appeared that the tender loving care was what did the trick. Further investigation, however, showed that this conclusion was typical of the usual approach of man, namely, looking at things from man's point of view. For closer observation showed that the handling each day was not a pleasurable experience. To the contrary, it was a frightening and stressful one. And, it appears now, it was the stress, the unpleasant part of the experience, that caused the test rats to develop larger brains and bodies! In some primitive societies, children, especially boys, are deliberately put through stressful, frightening experiences. Not only are these children apparently none the worse for it, but one study indicated that they were in better shape than those of a neighboring tribe in which physical conditions were similar.

The interaction of mind and body shows up in other ways as well. Experimental subjects have been "trained" to control those portions of their physical activities that have traditionally been called automatic—blood pressure, heartbeat, etc. If such responses can be controlled at will, it may in effect be possible to train patients with related types of disorders to get well.

Professor Krech sees the future of education thus:

> Both the biochemist and the teacher of the future will combine their skills and insights for the educational and intellectual development of the child. Tommy needs a bit more of an immediate memory stimulator; Jack could do with a

chemical attention-span stretcher; Rachel needs an anticho-
linesterase to slow down her mental processes; Joan, some
puromycin—she remembers too many details, and gets lost.

The ultimate—which does not seem very likely at the moment—will be knowledge pills and injections or perhaps EAI
(Electrically Assisted Instruction). Or, as science writer
Albert Rosenfeld put it, perhaps a virus can be developed
that will give us French instead of flu.

Even assuming, however, that this kind of thing can be
done, do not think for a moment that all will be clear sailing
from then on. "There is," says British science editor Nigel
Calder, "a rather hazy line between intervention to forestall
obvious congenital malformations and more general intervention to enchance the intelligence of all children, which could
produce a dangerous imbalance in society between intelligence and emotion." A similar charge has been leveled against
science and technology; that is to say, science and technology
have moved ahead faster than have our emotional and
political abilities to handle it. Or, as Professor Delgado puts
it, ". . . natural history teaches that when underdeveloped
brains are in charge of great power, the result is extinction."
A dangerous imbalance might also arise between a very bright
younger generation and a less bright older one. If you think
there is a generation gap now. . . .

And what will happen when, and if, we are able to make
substantial changes in people's personalities? Trying to change
the attitudes of adult and juvenile delinquents, as well as unhappy and maladjusted persons of all kinds, is fully accepted
today. What will happen when, and if, we in our greater
knowledge are really able to make basic changes in people's
personalities? Certainly criminals and psychopathic personalities will fall under the umbrella of biology and its chemical
and electrical control possibilities. Suppose a vicious killer
is caught and his personality is adjusted by drugs, surgery,

or ESB. Is he then the same person he was? Should he be punished? I suppose that one answer is that if society has this kind of capability, then the killer would probably never have gotten to that point to begin with. An optimistic thought.

Well, then, suppose that John Doe doesn't like being the quiet type; he's tired of always being the quiet one in the crowd. He goes and gets himself a personality adjustment. But Mary Doe married John because she liked him the way he was. What happens now?

Sir George Thomson, in his book *The Foreseeable Future*, went even further. He pondered the question of what would happen if scientists finally learned the secrets of the brain and mind. Is it possible, he asked, that we will not be able to maintain the values we cherish—such as friendship, honor, love, unselfishness—when (and if) we find them to be a particular grouping of electrons, or when we can express them in the form of circuit diagrams?

There are those, of course, who fervently believe that this will never happen. The great physicist Niels Bohr believed that the search for a molecular explanation of consciousness was a waste of time. He felt, and a number of others agree, that the brain may not be capable of understanding itself, that it requires something more complex and more clever than itself to accomplish this.

Let us see what this might be.

10

Mind and Machine

WE OFTEN EQUATE the eye of a TV camera with the human eye. Indeed, microminiaturization of electronic parts has progressed to the point where it may well be possible to build a TV camera small enough to be inserted into the eye socket of a blind person.

But our eyes do far more than simply record the scene in front of them. Similarly, our brains used to be thought of as a sort of receptacle into which all the senses simply poured their information. But it has been found that not only are there neural pathways coming from the senses to the brain, but there are also pathways carrying information from the brain to the senses. This information is used to increase or decrease the amount of information sent from the various senses at any one time to the brain. In this way the brain can control the rate of input to it. This, basically, is what we meant by "paying attention."

Auxiliary Senses

The idea of paying attention has built into it the collection by the senses of information from some external source and its delivery to the brain. But the means we have traditionally used to take in this information, namely, by looking, listening, etc., may be in for some changes.

For example, there are basically two ways to tape music from your radio or phonograph. One is to place a microphone in front of the loud-speaker; the other is to skip the external medium (air) and plug the signals right into the tape machine by taking the signals directly from the pre-amplifier or perhaps from taps on the speaker terminals.

When you watch television, you are doing the first. It has been calculated that less than 1 per cent of your retinal area is used in watching a typical TV screen. There is some feeling of realism, and if a play is really good you might forget that you are watching a small picture on a screen. But suppose you could plug—or be plugged—directly into the mechanism. The signals would pass directly from the origin—which could be anywhere—into your brain. You would be wherever the sensory mechanism is: Australia, the Arctic, at the ocean bottom, or even off in space.

And if the sensor is not so far away that it would take a long time for the signals to travel back and forth, a process of feedback could be used so that you could direct the sensor. That is, you could turn your head to the left, and the sensor—such as a sound-equipped color television camera—would do the same. By the time this can be done, the TV picture will undoubtedly be in 3-D. In other words, you can be there, yet still in the comfort and safety of your home or office.

If scientists could learn the electrochemical code that converts light rays into visual sensations in the brain, we could even give sight to the blind through the tiny TV camera we mentioned earlier, instead of just taking pictures with it. Similarly, the deaf could be made to hear. Another possibility is to replace the usual senses with some form of direct line to the brain via ESB. This could be a substitute for damaged

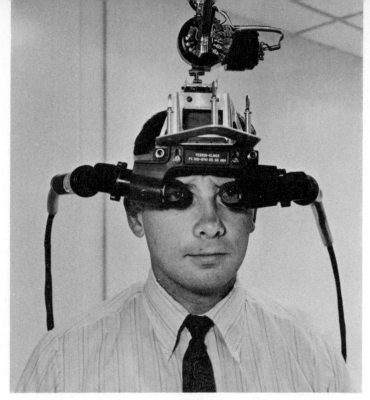

Experimental "head-mounted display unit" permits computer-generated pictures to be seen in three dimensions. Thus, an architect will be able to "see" the building he designs before it is built, and from any angle. In operation, cables from a computer transmit signals to cathode ray tubes (similar to television screens); pictures are projected in front of wearer's eyes by prisms. Device was created by Dr. I. Sutherland during research for Advanced Research Projects Agency, Department of Defense.

senses or a bonus for those with normal senses. According to author-scientist Arthur C. Clarke:

> One can imagine a time, when men who still inhabit organic bodies are regarded with pity by those who have passed on to an infinitely richer mode of existence, capable of throwing their consciousness or sphere of attention instantaneously to a point on land, sea or sky where there is a suitable sensing organ.

Artificial senses would enable us to do many other things we cannot do now. The sea, for example, is still largely unexplored. A big problem is that light does not penetrate water well, and so vision is extremely limited in the ocean depths. Clouds of sediment kicked up by submarine vehicles present another problem. Sound waves, however, travel very well through water and are not affected by murkiness. New work on a process called acoustical holography promises three-dimensional visual images from high-frequency sound waves. Using a similar system, dolphins and bats are known to navigate perfectly well even though blindfolded.

Other possible augmentations of the senses would be the ability to hear very low- or high-pitched sounds; "see" in the dark by use of infrared sensors as some snakes can; see some

New concept in Army helicopter fire control requires no mechanical link between pilot and cockpit. This gunsighting system automatically aims pre-selected guns wherever the operator looks. A Honeywell engineer sights through eyepiece of first production model helmet.

colors we normally cannot, as bees see by reflected ultra-violet light; or see polarized light or x-rays. We could also have built-in zoom lenses and filters.

Our sense of touch may also be involved. For instance, wearers of artificial limbs sometimes have the problem of not really knowing how much pressure they are exerting when they pick something up. Since the maximum pressure they can exert is relatively small, they usually don't have to worry about breaking things. On the other hand, if the hold is not tight enough, the object may begin to slip out of the hand before the wearer gets a visual clue and can do something about it. Dr. Fred Leonard of the Walter Reed Army Medical Center has therefore suggested the inclusion of a "slippage detector" on the grasping digits. The detector is a piezoelectric crystal such as that used in a small phonograph where the crystal converts the mechanical vibration of the needle into an electrical signal. Thus as the object begins to slip in the artificial hand, it would generate a signal that could be used to automatically tighten the grip.

By combining such visual, aural, and touch sensors with specially built teleoperators, a physician anywhere in the world would be able to examine a patient who is miles away. Not only would he be able to see the patient, and listen to his heart and lungs, but with the force feedback we talked of in the manipulators, he could even feel for swellings and perform other diagnostic techniques dependent on the sense of touch.

Another fascinating possibility is remote-control dentistry. I am sure that each of us has experienced the discomfort that occurs when the dentist tries to get his big hand into our small mouth, and of the awkward positions required of both the dentist and the patient.

Dr. I. J. Good, author and consultant, has proposed the idea of remote-control dentistry. He points out that the dentist "would be able to work sitting down . . . and he would become less tired and would make fewer mistakes. . . . His accuracy could be improved still further if the (stereoscopic) image of the mouth could be larger than the real mouth. In fact the size could even be variable, going right up to the size of a room." Gone would be the boring statement, "Open wide," and that occupational hazard of dentists, fallen arches.

In a similar manner, a surgeon could be "inside" the body when he operates. Already a bronchoscope has been developed that provides a color TV picture of the inside of a patient's respiratory (breathing) system. The size of the surgeon's incision could probably be reduced in many cases. (There is a mathematical relationship talked of in medical circles that tells us that the length of the incision is directly proportional to the size of the surgeon's hand.)

For extremely delicate surgery, a *micro*manipulator is a natural; and it can damp the natural tremor of even the best surgeon's hands. Moreover, the surgeon could operate from anywhere in the world.

Computers

We said in an earlier chapter that computers can handle many of man's mental jobs. Indeed, computers are becoming more and more a part of the way we think, the way we act, and the way we make decisions. Already a large field of effort has developed that deals with how best to match man and computer—how to ask the computer questions or put in instructions and information, and how best to get the answers or data back to man for whom, generally, the effort has been made. This work is being done largely by engineers, by psychologists, and by biologists. Dr. D. C. Englebart of the Stanford Research Institute points out, for instance, "You build a system, use it for a while, then all of a sudden find that a

Pattern Recognition Computer (PRC) at Cornell Aeronautical Laboratory is employed in research on new computer techniques. Special purpose computer is able to recognize and distinguish various types of patterns such as letters of the alphabet, images in a photograph or numbers. It can also be taught to recognize speech sounds.

man gets a backache having to use a light pen all day in a new way." He refers here to the relatively new process of communicating with a computer by "writing" on a vertical television-like screen with a light pen.

In another example provided by Dr. Englebart, communication with the computer was by typewriter keyboard. The computer program called for the flexibility of being able to insert and delete words that were flashed on the screen, both by the computer and as the operator typed on the keyboard. To do this a dot was positioned under a particular word and a *dw* (delete word) button was pushed, or an *rw* (replace word) button. The question was how best to place or control the movement of this *tracking spot*. Some of the more common solutions are a light pen, a joy stick similar to

148

that used for controlling a light plane, and turning knobs
(one for up/down, one for left/right).

The Stanford Research Institute's solution is an interesting
one, and consists of a small control unit that rests on wheels
on the bottom of a box. The wheels are set up in such a way
that moving the box left and right does the same with the
tracking spot; movement forward and backward is equivalent
to up and down motion on the screen. The control box, which
has the *rw* and *dw* buttons on it, was nicknamed the "mouse,"
and is therefore clearly a biological solution!

Another way of communicating with the computer is verb-
ally. This technique is in the process of development now.

**The "mouse" is used to help the operator communicate
with a computer. Held in the operator's right hand, it
positions a tracking spot on a cathode ray tube face.
Device under left hand provides one-handed entry into
the computer.**

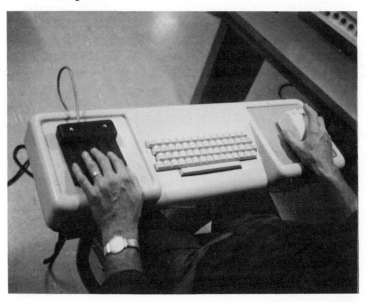

149

With a radio built into the ear, this conversation could take place even when the operator is not in the computer's presence. Something similar is already in wide operation, namely, telephone connection between keyboard operator and computer.

But the future is likely to see a much greater intimacy develop than even this. Perhaps a radio or microwave receiver-transmitter will be installed in the operator's brain. If it is sensitive enough, and if we can decode the brain's electrical activities, then, in a manner reminiscent of EMG control, signals can flow almost uninterruptedly between operator and computer at the speed of light.

Signals could also flow between operator and android. Here is a possible application, as foreseen by Samuel Delaney in his science fiction novel, *Nova**:

* Doubleday, 1968, p. 75.

> Neither he (Lorq) nor his father had seen his mother in person for four years. Victim of a degenerative mental and physical disease that often left her totally incommunicative, she had retired to her suite in the house with her medicines, her diagnostic computers, her cosmetics, her gravothermy and reading machines. She—or more often one of her androids programmed to her general response pattern—would appear in the viewing columns and present a semblance of her normal appearance and personality. In the same way, through android and telerama report, she 'accompanied' Von Ray on his business travels, while her physical presence was confined in the masked, isolate chambers that no one was allowed to enter except the psychotechnician who came quietly once a month.

Another approach is to "plug in" to the computer. This is not a new idea, although no one has any idea as yet of how to accomplish it. Normally it means that man plugs somehow into the computer. But Delaney, again in his science fiction novel, sees it the other way. The operator is fitted with sockets in his wrists, small of the back, ankles, and back of the neck. When the spaceship or other computer is plugged into him, nervous impulses from his body provide the required directions to the computer.

The implication in all of this is that of a "mutual aid society." * Neither man nor machine (computer) is able to accomplish alone what they can in combination.

And if one man and one computer can accomplish a lot, think of what can be done if several men and computers can be linked together—somehow. Dr. Englebart uses the analogy of a group of men framing a house. (Sometimes houses are not built as a unit; rather, the four sides are built separately and then raised into place.) He points out (referring to the possibility of linking multiple consoles) that the men who raise the four frames into place can see each other through the frames and so coordinate their efforts. Without this ability their job would be far more difficult. Already, man has created a sort of supermemory by means of his books, pictures, and museums.

We may yet see another, quite different combination of mind and machine. For one thing, it may not be economically feasible to build the extraordinarily complex computers that will eventually evolve, even if it is technically possible. Hence we may find it necessary to "grow" them, or perhaps to "grow" the proper connections by "teaching" the machine, as a child is taught. Perhaps something of the brain's complexity can be approached by taking a very direct approach—using a culture of brain cells instead of electronic components.

It is worth noting, however, that the great computer pioneer John von Neumann once figured out that electronic cells could be far more efficient than living ones; already they are much faster. In either case, whether it be living or electronic cells, it is the complexity that tells the tale and creates the

* In nature, this is called *symbiosis*.

possibilities. Already, we see eerie possibilities. Dr. D. E. Wooldridge—author, professor, and businessman—feels that "we must keep an open mind as to the possibility that among the wires and transistors of existing electronic computers, there already flickers the dim glimmering of some kind of personal awareness. . . ."

William Blake once wrote:

> Naught loves another as itself,
> Nor venerates another so,
> Nor is it possible to Thought
> A greater than itself to know. . . .

But that was in the seventeenth century, before the days of computers. Is it possible that man, with the aid of his machines, will someday unravel the deepest secret of the universe, the essence of thought?

11

Biotechnology

MODERN MAN, AND especially the city dweller, has come to equate biology with medicine; he is mainly concerned with what might be called "skin-in" biology, and tends to ignore a large group of fields that can be grouped under "skin-out" biology. Sanitation, plant genetics, animal husbandry, environmental control, ecology,* and many others are all very much the concern of biology.

Biochemical production is already an important aspect of our industrial empire. Drugs, sera, and vaccines are produced in huge quantities. Most industrial enzymes—such as those that are revolutionizing the detergent industry—are produced by bacteria, not machines. Indeed, we may find sometime in the future that photosynthesis has been taken out of the "hands" of plants and reproduced artificially by machine. We may see biochemical machines for food production, energy transformation, chemical manufacturing, and information storage. Already there are synthetic food products on the market. It is

* Ecology is the study of the relation of plants and animals to their environment. The 22nd Annual Brookhaven Biology Symposium, held in 1969, was devoted to "Diversity and Stability in Ecological Systems."

worth noting that biochemical methods, being more complex and versatile, can use cheaper and less pure starting materials than can purely chemical methods. Living cells, or some derivative thereof, may one day be used to supply manufacturing instructions via DNA or RNA to our biological machines, such as one that will perform the first stages of extraction of ore from oceans.

Supplying enough energy to meet the world's growing needs

Photosynthesis may one day be carried on outside the cell. Dr. J. A. Bassham demonstrates apparatus for isolating spinach chloroplasts (the tiny "factories" in which photosynthesis takes place).

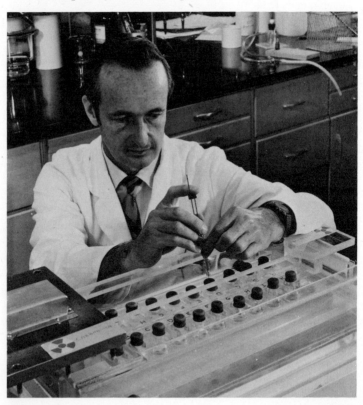

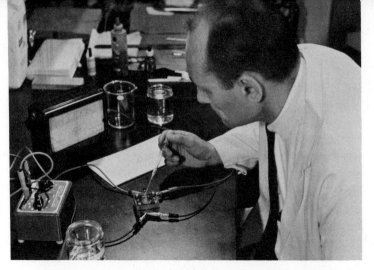

Harold Warner, chief of the Emory University Yerkes Regional Primate Research Center, is working on a fuel cell capable of generating electricity from the chemical energy in glucose, a sugar found in plants and animals. The fuel cell could use body fluids to power implanted cardiac pacemakers or other prostheses and, perhaps, when the time comes, artificial hearts. Most pacemakers are now powered by batteries which have to be replaced at least once every two years, with surgery necessary.

is becoming more and more of a problem. Researchers at Emory University are wondering about the possibilities of utilizing the energy locked up in the chemical bonds of plants. How about, they suggest, a lawn mower that can operate from its own clippings?

In short, man lives in a biological world, though from the way he acts you would hardly think so. The city dweller, particularly, tends to think that he lives in a totally artificial world. His food comes in packages from the supermarket and not from plants and animals; his energy comes from a socket in the wall and not from a dwindling supply of biologically derived coal and oil; his furniture comes from the furniture store and not from trees; his wastes go down the drain and into a sewer, not into a world of which he is still a part.

This biological world is called the *biosphere,* by analogy

with the atmosphere, ionosphere, and hydrosphere, and consists of the world of living things—from the simplest one-celled creatures to the higher animals. We shall have to be rather more aware of the biosphere from now on. For we have taken advantage of it, ignored it, ravaged it. Just as a man who mistreats his body tends to ignore it until it begins to give him trouble, we have done the same with our Earth. Now there are signs of sickness and disease.

It has long been known that a man cannot pour poisons into his body without negative results; we are only just finding that our Earth reacts the same way. We saw in the last few chapters that man and machine are becoming more closely linked every day. But man's link with Earth has gone on since his creation. Looking at the Earth from its surface, or even from a few thousand feet up, it seems infinitely large and capable of dealing with any punishment we can hand out. But the astronauts have gotten a different view; from far out in space the Earth looks lost and lonely in a sea of space—fragile, almost, as indeed we are finding it to be. More than one scientist has even stated, seriously, that if man continues along as he has been going, he may make his home totally unlivable in a generation or two. In other words, he will by ignorance, greed, and stupidity succeed in doing what aggression, brutality, and force have not succeeded in doing. And that is to wipe himself off the face of the Earth.

Strong words. Perhaps even exaggerated. But is it worth taking the chance?

Every minute of the day and night, our nation pours 120 million gallons of sewage and other kinds of waste materials into its waterways. President Johnson said in 1967 that every major river system in the United States is polluted. Some of this pollution is automatically cleaned up by the natural processes of filtration, sedimentation, oxidation, and bacterial attack.

156

But the condition of a river, lake, or ocean is rather like that of a sick human. If not too sick, and allowed to recuperate, it will do so. The cleaning-up operation is equivalent to our bodies' antidisease process. If it is overwhelmed, however, death results.

Sometimes the person, or the water system, just remains sick. Thus there are all levels of pollution. Along the Hudson River in New York State, for instance, the condition of the river ranges from being suitable for drinking in its upper reaches, through suitable for bathing along the middle portion, to being both disgusting and poisonous around and near New York City.

When the amount of polluting material goes beyond the natural capability of the water to clean itself up, the undesirable forms of life like algae take over, using up all the oxygen in the water and making it unlivable and unusable to other living things. Chemicals, including the phosphates in laundry detergents, also combine with the oxygen in the water.

Sludge from New York City is barged out a few miles and dumped into the Atlantic Ocean, resulting in a 20-square-mile "dead sea." This, in a region that once abounded with sea life.

It was once thought—I once thought—that the world's seas were infinitely vast. Yet certain species of whale have been hunted to extinction; and the greatest, most magnificent living thing on Earth, the blue whale, is coming ever closer to that point. Clearly the seas are not infinitely vast.

Clearly, too, if we can kill off a small area of ocean—and we have done this to the whole of Lake Erie and to many rivers as well—then we may even be able to do it to the whole ocean if we try hard enough. Should we manage to turn the teeming oceans into dead seas, we shall surely be adding to the dangers of human extinction.

And, as you have surely heard, we are polluting our air and filling the land with solid wastes as well. We won't go into any details here, except to point out that what is needed is a view of the Earth as being potentially destructible and unlivable. Once we become conscious of this—and there are hopeful signs—we will stop fouling our nest."

We must try to find ways to cut down on the flood of waste material we are sending into our air, water, and land. One way, of course, is to cut down on the number of people who are creating the pollution. While an important objective, the problems are immense and there seems little likelihood that we will see even a slowing down of the rapidly increasing population of the Earth.

A major step, and one somewhat more likely to be achieved, is to stop, and perhaps reverse, the increasing trend to pre-package everything and to make everything disposable and non-returnable—bottles, cans, individually packaged slices of cheese, and so on.

Or, if this cannot be done, then the packaging materials must be made such that they will disintegrate when disposed of, and go back into the Earth's storehouse of raw materials. One of the problems is that plastics are a recent invention, and so microorganisms that have learned to attack and degrade most other forms of organic matter have not had time to develop an appetite for plastics.

For example, many plants will die if doused with kerosene or motor oil. And the effects of oil slicks on ocean life have become only too well known. Yet there are types of bacteria that find certain petroleum products quite suitable for a luncheon treat. What they are doing is breaking down the oil into its harmless constituents, such as carbon, oxygen, and hydrogen. They are degrading it. The oil, in other words, is biodegradable. With more and better sewage-treatment plants, such microorganisms can be given more of a chance to do their work.

158

We could go even further. John Maynard Smith, of Great Britain, suggests that "perhaps we shall learn to synthesize the necessary DNA sequences and incorporate them into our domestic animals to enable them to browse on and digest the nylon and polyethylene which we may expect by then to cover England to a depth of several feet." Nylon and polyethylene, you see, are non-biodegradable. Thus we must either develop organisms that can break down plastic films, packages, and bottles, or develop plastics that will degrade. The Japanese, for example, have proposed and are working on a biodegradable "glass" bottle, one that could be broken down by soil bacteria into, hopefully, nutrients for the soil.

We must, in other words, begin to change our way of thinking. For one thing, we always seem to make the wrong things long-lasting. Our cars seem to be designed to break down within a few years after they are built—but to last for decades when discarded, as some 7 million are each year in the United States.

Pesticides

A similar problem, unfortunately, has arisen with our major pesticides, or bug killers. This problem too arose as a result of our short-sighted view of things. The now infamous DDT achieved an enviable and deserved reputation as effective, cheap, and long-lasting when it began to be widely used just before World War II. The fact that it was long-lasting means that you didn't have to keep applying it, which was also why it was cheap. That meant it kept on working, and working, and working—even after you didn't want it to. It also meant that the poison didn't break down inside the body of the insect it killed, but remained intact to kill the bird that ate the insect, and remained to enter the bloodstream of the person or animal that ate the bird. And it remained to go back into the Earth and perhaps into the water system of a nearby community. It has been estimated that of some 1.5 million tons of the material produced, perhaps two-thirds of it is still active, strictly because of the fact that it is not biodegradable. The average American now has about twelve parts per million of DDT in his fatty tissues.

Things that are long-lasting are not always desirable.

This is not meant to criticize the use of pesticides. They are important, indeed, vital. Vast numbers of people go to bed hungry each night. (This, unfortunately, is as much a problem of uneven distribution as it is of any food shortages.) And in spite of incredible advances in food production, the situation may very well be getting worse, not better. Dr. Lloyd V. Berkner—author, scientist, and administrator—figures that the world food supply has been rising at an average rate of 1 per cent a year, while world population rises at a rate of 1.8 per cent, or almost twice as fast.*

Unfortunately, ever-increasing numbers of people will mean ever-decreasing amounts of land available for cultivation, which in turn will mean an ever-increasing need for pesticides, insecticides, chemical fertilizers, etc. Unless something drastic is done, we are liable to end up in an ever-tightening circle of chemical contamination in which we must fight the effects of an excess of chemicals with more chemicals.

Another important point to be made is that no animal can exist on its own waste products. Yet, as E. L. Yochelson pointed out in a letter to *Science* magazine, "Every movement toward changing the world to a place for man to the exclusion of other living organisms leads to this end. A world aimed at being exclusively ours will be a world in which man cannot survive."

One of the two major threats to the food supply (aside from unequal distribution between the rich and poor people) is

* Other estimates of world population growth are even higher. In either case, with the death rate falling and the birth rate likely to remain about the same, the population growth rate may well rise to 3 per cent a year.

pests; the other is disease. The losses from these two are immense. It has been estimated that one-fifth of the principal food grains, upon which most of the world's population depends, is lost to insects and disease. In the 1940's a plant disease struck the rice crop in India. As a direct result, more than a million people died.

But chemicals, even short-lived ones, are not the only remedy. There are a number of biological answers that will be used more and more as time goes on. In the case of the plant disease just mentioned, a remarkable example of genetic engineering changed the characteristics of the rice crop; this made it immune to the disease, which had been a recurring one. There was another rice plant that had good resistance to the disease but which was not as satisfactory in other ways. A small section of the chromosome that gave this other plant its resistance was transferred to the more popular plant, thus making it immune too.

Another genetic approach is to increase the yield per acre of the crop plant. This of course goes beyond simply using good farming methods, irrigation, and fertilizer. It means changing the characteristics of the plant so that it can take up large amounts of fertilizer which make it grow faster and perhaps larger. Thus it is possible to grow two or three crops a year where only one or two could be grown before. Heat tolerance can be built in to permit summer growth. The leaves can be made to stand out, rather than droop, to permit maximum absorption of sunlight and photosynthesis. The stalks can be made shorter or longer so that more of the useful part grows. The stalks can also be made stiffer to facilitate machine harvesting.

The list is almost endless. And the results, wherever this has been tried, are startling. In 1943 Mexico produced eleven bushels of wheat per acre and had to import half its needs. Twenty years later, it was producing thirty-seven bushels per acre. In spite of a growing population, it had some for export.

Daniel Sarria, chief of corn research at the Palmira station of the Colombian Institute of Agriculture, uses
light table to separate out dark kernels of opaque-2
corn for breeding experiments. Experiments on fatten-
ing pigs have shown opaque-2 to be 30 per cent more
efficient than the normal diet.

The same story can be told for rice in the Philippines, in
India, and various other parts of the world. This is not to
say that the food problem has been solved, even in these
countries. The new methods are expensive and the small
farmer often cannot afford them. And, as in our country, which
produces far more than it needs, there are hungry people
because of problems of distribution, poverty, and the like.

Nevertheless, the promise is great enough that the change
has been called a "green revolution." And Professor S. S.
Chase, of The State University of New York and Harvard,
feels that "genetic engineering of the major food grains is
one of the most exciting things man is doing today."

Another possibility into which plant geneticists are looking is the creation or adaptation of edible plants or animals that can thrive on the wastes we throw away. The key word here is *recycling*. We mentioned earlier that certain bacteria thrive on some petroleum products. Perhaps edible materials, such as yeasts, seaweed, plankton, or even bacteria can be developed to both add to the world food supply and reduce pollution.

A lesson has been learned, in other words, from the space program. When the astronauts go up, they are cut off from Earth. On long trips they cannot afford the luxuries we have become used to on Earth, such as fresh foods and water and carelessly discarding their wastes. Food, oxygen, and wastes are all resources that must be conserved. Already energy is produced, along with water, from fuel cells that "burn" hydrogen and oxygen. It is known that urine can be purified back into drinking water without a great deal of trouble. Experiments are in progress to see whether the astronauts' solid wastes can be utilized as fuel for the fuel cells, or perhaps even as some sort of rocket fuel. On long trips, it will certainly have to be used as a nutrient for some form of growing food supply for the astronauts, such as an edible algae that is being

Bacteria (tiny rod-shaped objects) shown digesting waste cellulose and converting it into microbial protein.

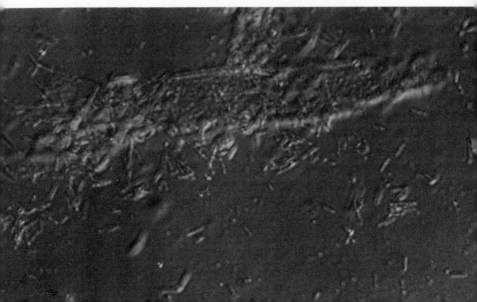

grown on board the craft. It is not a complete coincidence that our globe has been called "spaceship earth."

Specialists in plant genetics are considering the possibility of breeding plants for high levels of amino acids or proteins instead of the more usual, and less valuable, carbohydrates. In some cases, useless but prolific plants in tropical areas can be transformed into good crop plants.

Various forms of genetic control are also being experimented with in insect control. One form that has already been tried with success is the so-called sterile-male technique. Males of the offending insect are raised in large numbers and then sterilized by means of chemicals or radiation. Since many types of insect mate only once, the non-fertile males "use up" the reproductive ability of large numbers of the females. Over a period of several generations, the numbers of the pest can be reduced drastically. This was accompanied in Florida with the screwworm fly. Such means are admittedly far more expensive than chemical means. But, says Dr. E. F. Knipling of the U.S. Department of Agriculture, "The cost of eradicating screwworm fly from Florida [in this way] was about $8,000,000, but the accrued savings to the livestock industry over the last 10 years have been variously estimated to range from $100,000,000 to $700,000,000." And, of course, there is not the problem of poisoning other species (including man) as well.

Unexpected Results

It is well to remember, however, that insects feed on, and are fed on by, other living things. These will be affected in some way by the disappearance of the insect. There is also the danger that the "hole" left by this particular species will be occupied by another, even more pestiferous one. It may be necessary, therefore, to introduce a harmless insect type that fits into the chain.

This is an aspect of natural biology that is extraordinarily tricky and that is only now being given its proper measure of attention. I refer here to what has come to be called *ecological balance.* As we mentioned earlier, the word ecology refers to the relations of living things to their surroundings. In many areas the ecology can be said to be only precariously balanced. Sometimes it may not take much to upset it and an imported species may not always do what is expected of it. Indeed, when man once begins to "monkey" with the ecology of a region, all kinds of catastrophes can happen.

An animal that has often been at the center of controversy along these lines is the humble rabbit. Its rapid breeding habits make it seem like a good bet in places that are short of meat. Further, its hair can be used to make felt. And rabbits' feet are believed by some to bring good luck.

But when rabbits are introduced into a new region, chaos can result. In one case, they practically cleaned an island of what had once been a beautiful green cover. Then, to compound the problem, they made so many burrows under the ground that the inhabitants had to be careful as they walked because the ground was continually falling in. Even the houses began to tip here and there as they were undermined by the rabbit burrows.

How to get rid of them? The complications are well described in a book called *The Alien Animals,* by George Laycock. I quote from one section on rabbits:

> One of the most involved and unpredictable sequences of events in the history of rabbit transplanting was reported by the French naturalist Roger Heim. Rabbits were introduced to the Macquarie Islands, far to the southwest of New Zealand, to provide food. They were shortly competing with sheep, however, and farmers began looking about for a cure to the rabbit problem. The cat appeared to hold promise. So cats were turned loose to eat the rabbits. But the cats turned to eating sea birds. This was bad because sea-bird eggs were an important food for the native people.

The cure for the cat appeared to be the dog, so dogs were turned loose. To the surprise of the planners, however, the dogs neglected the cats in preference to the seals, also an important source of human food. There was little the wildlife manipulators could do then except admit that the dogs had not controlled the cats that had not controlled the rabbits that seemed so desirable at the beginning.

On a larger scale, the continent of Australia was similarly bedeviled for almost a century. Here, in one attempt to get rid of the imported rabbits, a natural predator of the animal, the fox, was introduced. Unfortunately, the foxes became more interested in the slower marsupials (creatures like kangaroos, which carry their young around in pouches) that haven't been doing too well as it is.

Yet, incredible as it may seem, in the early 1950's this same European rabbit, which had been known to be a veritable plague in many parts of the world, was introduced into Ohio and Pennsylvania by hunters who were looking for new game!

Insect Control

It is interesting to note that some measure of control over the rabbit infestation in Australia was finally achieved through use of a virus, *Myxomatosis cuniculi*. It turns out that viruses are being proposed for control of a number of insect pests as well. In the Pacific Northwest, the tussock moth destroys millions of board feet of fir timber. Scientists have found a virus that appears to attack only this moth and are working on the possibilities of controlling it in this way.

Thus far the U.S. Food and Drug Administration is still not sure about this method and wants further proof that the viruses will not be harmful to other animal life, including man. The prospect seems good. Although no one expects this to be *the* answer to the insect problem, *Science News* maga-

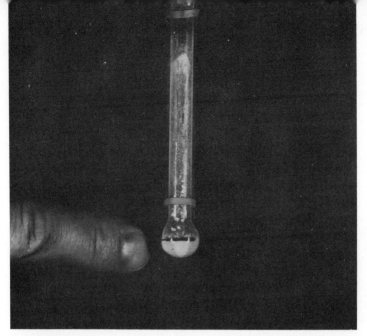

Less than an eyedropper of virus material, shown at the bottom of this test tube, can control a specific insect population on ten acres of land.

zine reports that "Insect pathologists think they may be able to develop specific viruses against each of at least 10 of the major insect pests."

But insects breed quickly and strains of them have been able to develop that are immune to almost anything man has been able to do to them. Thus we have the ironic situation where such pesticides as DDT are still poisoning other species, while the insects they were meant to control begin to proliferate all over again.

There is, however, a different biological approach to insect control that might be even more specific and foolproof. The control of insect metamorphosis from one stage to the next depends upon a substance that has been named *juvenile hormone*. As long as juvenile hormone is flowing in the insect it will continue to grow. When the hormone, which is different for each insect, stops flowing, then metamorphosis takes place. In insect control, the hormone is applied at the wrong time, resulting in a derangement of the life cycle, and hence the insects die before they are able to reproduce. It is extremely unlikely that the insects will be able to develop an immunity to the treatment, since it is a normal chemical found in their own bodies. Very tiny amounts have been found to be quite effective, although even large doses have been found to be harmless to other animal species—or even to other insects!

Though these biological approaches to insect control seem rather complex and specialized, there is no question but that they will have to be pursued, regardless of the economics. That this is indeed happening is shown by a comparison of effort at the entomology (insect) research division of the Department of Agriculture. In 1955 insecticides took 65 per cent of the division's attention. In 1968 that figure had dropped to 16 per cent, while biological controls had risen to 51 per cent from a very small amount in the earlier time.

Yet other approaches are possible. Male cockroaches are attracted to young females who emit a substance with a particular odor. If this substance can be produced synthetically, large numbers of just this species can be lured to their death. Other insects, not considered pests by man, would be spared.

In 1939, the British author H. G. Wells, along with J. S. Huxley and G. P. Wells, wrote a book called *The Science of Life*, a remarkable compendium of much that was known at the time about the subject. Toward the end of the long book there is a particularly intriguing statement:

> Perhaps no man has yet imagined what a forest may some day be, a forest of great trees without disease, free of stinging insect or vindictive reptile, open, varied and delightful. The wilderness will become a world-garden and the desert a lonely resort for contemplation and mental refreshment. An enormous

range of possibility in the selective breeding of plants and animals still remains to be explored.* One may doubt the need to exterminate even the wolf and tiger. The tiger may cease to be the enemy of man and his cattle; the wolf, bred and subdued, may crouch at his feet.

In a sense, what we have been discussing in this chapter is environmental control. For everything about us is the environment, and there seems little doubt that man's history is one of ever greater control over it.

But environmental control has some nasty connotations. And perhaps the word ecology is a better one, implying as it does maintaining a balance, rather than exerting forcible control. Another advantage to ecology is that it takes biologists out of their sterile, man-made laboratories and into the world of nature. Here they must look at plants and animals as part of the biosphere, and not as man-controlled, or even man-made.

Someday man may indeed produce all his food in factories, and have all wild animals at his feet. My own feeling is that we will have lost something beautiful and valuable if it should happen.

* Will we one day have straight bananas with a square cross-section to facilitate packing?

12

Summing Up

It has been reported in *Science* magazine that 10 to 18 per cent of hospitalized patients who receive drugs develop reactions to them, some of which are very dangerous.

Does this mean, as some would suggest, that we must abandon the use of drugs? Clearly not, unless we are willing to return to the days when we were at the mercy of such infectious diseases as tuberculosis, smallpox, diphtheria, and typhoid.

Much more satisfactory would be either a better knowledge of the action of the drugs and who is allergic to them, or perhaps better drugs. In either case, what is necessary is more, not less, science. Perhaps better science, perhaps more concerned or enlightened science, but not a decrease.

Along with those who unthinkingly condemn all medical drugs are the ones who maintain that man's technological capability has outrun his sociological or humanistic capability. They may be right. But their solution—to stop all science and technology in its tracks—is not only impractical, it is approaching the problem backwards. What they feel is that new developments will be put to improper use. But, as an editorial in *The New York Times* points out:

> The dilemma is not new. The first men to discover how to make fire must have realized soon afterward what a dangerous weapon they had forged, an understanding shared much later by those who introduced airplanes, nuclear fission and DDT.
> All new scientific and technological capability has the potential for evil as well as for good. But the biological fire which the molecular biologists promise to provide mankind is the most powerful knowledge conceivable. . . .

This is what has the anti-scientists really worried. The ones who feel most strongly about this—but don't think for a moment that scientists are not worried too—are sometimes called "humanists,*" and profess to value the human being over the machine and technology. This is ironic to an extreme degree, for the solution they (or some of them) propose is to turn away from science and rationality. Dr. R. L. Sinsheimer, however, suggests that "those who feel this way are not among the losers in that chromosomal lottery that so firmly channels our destinies."

"This response," he continues, "does not come from the 250,000 children born each year in this country with structural or functional defects. . . . It does not include, for example, the 50 million 'normal' Americans with an I.Q. of less than 90." In other words, you may be sure that not a single one of these "losers" will argue that the work being done by biologists is dangerous and should be stopped.

Burying our heads in the sand is certainly not the answer. The absurdity of the "stop science" approach can be seen clearly in Samuel Butler's book, *Erewhon,* written in 1872. In this fictional civilization, all inventions that had been discovered in the preceding 271 years were destroyed. Thus a visitor, who is carrying a *watch*, is considered a suspicious

* This is only one of several meanings for the term "humanist," which has literary and religious meanings as well.

character and possible subversive. Even worse, in the eyes of the Erewhonians, is being sick, which they consider the worst kind of "crime."

In the early 1800's a group called the Luddites blamed a period of economic distress on the introduction of machines to the process of manufacturing. Their answer was to destroy the machines, which they then went about doing, causing a great deal of damage in the process and keeping the regions involved in a continual state of disturbance. What is most interesting is that with the return of prosperity the riots ceased almost immediately.

Nor does it make sense to say that science is okay but machinery, i.e., technology, is not. Modern medical (or any) science would not be possible without "machines." A modern operating room is so crowded with sensitive detection, life-support, and other types of equipment that there is hardly room for the surgeon and his assistants.

So you see that it is not the new developments in science and technology that constitute the danger, but what society does with them. Indeed, this is really the heart of the matter.

Dr. H. B. Glass, of The State University of New York, says that "Only a prolonged and profound attention by many of the wisest men of our time [can] achieve a wise and sober solution of the crisis evoked in our world by scientific discoveries and their applications."

And Joshua Lederberg, Nobel Prize winner and Professor of Genetics at Stanford University, feels that "The most exciting and creative prospect for the 70's is a convergence of the scientific potency of molecular biology with the concern for human well-being of the environmental conservation movement."

A significant step along the way has been taken with the formation of a Council for Biology in Human Affairs. Twenty-five scientists, including five Nobel Prize winners, have formed

172

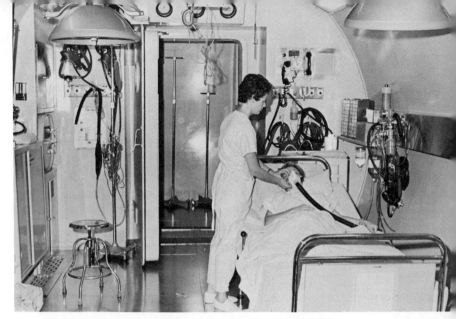

The hyperbaric chamber is used for the patient who
has trouble getting enough oxygen in a normal manner.
A high-pressure atmosphere "drives" the oxygen into
the blood.

the organization to try to forsee the possible consequences of
scientific developments, especially in biology.

The problem is that we can never do merely one thing. The
simplest development can have possible consequences that
are extremely difficult to detect early in the game. We have
seen what can happen when an animal is introduced into a
region. Here is another, perhaps less obvious example. Thanks
to the germ theory of disease, due largely to Pasteur, the biological and medical sciences have been able to fight disease
on many fronts, ranging from inoculation to better sanitation.
As a result, we are relatively free of infectious diseases. The
happy result is that millions of people who once might have
died from infectious diseases are saved; the unhappy result
is a population explosion that threatens to become a world
catastrophe. Putting it very simply, then, we shall have to be
very careful how we apply our science.

173

The Next Revolution?

Clearly the germ theory of disease has wrought one major revolution, and molecular genetics a second. Are there any developments on the horizon that hold promise of another basic revolution in biology? That is difficult to predict. But there is an interesting conjecture by Dr. Albert Szent-Györgyi, Nobel Laureate and researcher at the Marine Biological Laboratory in Massachusetts. Dr. Szent-Györgyi points out that the progress of biology has been marked by a shift toward smaller dimensions. In the eighteenth century biology was limited to structures that were visible with the naked eye; by the nineteenth it had descended to the cellular level; and by the twentieth the spotlight had dwindled to molecular size.

But, says Dr. Szent-Györgyi, "this outlook leads to a static world in which the main factors are bond angles and distances, and the main motion is the motion of clumsy macromolecules [i.e., large molecules] pushed about by random heat agitation. It does not explain the subtlety of biological reactions."

Dr. Szent-Györgyi suggests that we may be able to take another step down, into the electronic realm. There is evidence, he suggests, that a process called *charge transfer* is one of the most basic and common reactions, and one which connects the various parts of the same molecules and connects the different molecules to a more or less continuous electronic system. He has written:

> Such electronic transitions seem to dominate the physical state of the living cell. They may also underly the regulations of cellular activity, including the regulation of cell division, and are leading to a new theory of cancer. The electronic outlook may open the way to the approach of the major unsolved biological problems, like the mechanism of drug and hormone reaction, the mechanism of energy transformations,

and the nature of the reaction underlying learning and memory.

The next forward stride of biology, which will dominate this science in the twenty-first century, will be a shift from the molecular level to the electronic dimension.

Thus we have one candidate for a biological revolution. If we now look up the ladder of life, rather than down, we see yet other possibilities. Dr. George R. Harrison, in his book *What Man May Be*, wrote:

> Thus far, nucleons on earth have been able to swing into the patterns that form atoms, the atoms into molecules, the molecules into crystals and cells, and the cells into plant and animal creatures. In many of these creatures sensation and emotion and reason and imagination and spiritual aspiration have begun to develop. Societies of ever higher types, from termite and ant colonies to the United Nations, are formed. What further patterns may not arise. . . ?

The eminent theologian and author P. Teilhard de Chardin saw human evolution as moving toward what he called The Point Omega. This is "a harmonized collectivity of consciousness, equivalent to a kind of superconsciousness. The earth is covering itself not merely by myriads of thinking units, but by a single continuum of thought, and finally forming a functionally single Unit of Thought of planetary dimensions. . . ." *

Already, it should be pointed out, the life of an individual is far richer as a part of a larger society than it is in solitude. Perhaps experiences beyond our conception lie in store for our descendants.

This "larger life" may of course never come to be. Yet clearly some better form of cooperation among men and nations is required than what we have seen to date. Should it not come, then there is likely to arise a major alternative to the future of biology as I have sketched it; and that is

* In 1880, someone by the name of W. Preyer suggested that the Earth long, long ago was a single mighty organism.

that there may be no biology at all in the future. Through some form of insanity, such as nuclear war, or carelessness, such as accidental release of some biological agent, man may wipe himself right off the face of the Earth.

Some, who have been soured by what they have seen and perhaps experienced, may suggest that this might be all to the good; that clearly this experiment of nature, man, has been a huge mistake; that nature, God, or what have you should go back and try again. And if it takes another several million years, well, so be it.

Most of us, of course, feel differently. And if things are far from good for many, they are good for some, and in some ways are getting better. More important, man has, for the first time in his history, the potential to improve the conditions of the entire human race, or to destroy it. This is an awesome power, and one that should be handled carefully.

The more fearful insist that there are things better left unknown, that in tampering with viruses, for example, we might unleash an epidemic of disastrous proportions. The obvious answer, which we have already given, is that if scientists had taken that approach in the past, we would still be at the mercy of dozens of dread diseases. A hundred years ago, fully one-third of all children born failed to reach maturity.

But even more, can anyone honestly expect scientists not to try to open doors as they come to them? For scientists are, after all, only men. And when men stop rising to the challenge of the unknown, biology will have taken a completely new turn. For men will no longer be men, but something else entirely.

And this is also possible.

Bibliography

BOOKS

Beadle, G. and M., *The Language of Life; An Introduction to the Science of Genetics*, Doubleday, 1966.

Berger, M., *Famous Men of Modern Biology*, T. Y. Crowell, 1968.

————, *Tools of Modern Biology*, T. Y. Crowell, 1970.

Bernal, J. D., *The Origin of Life*, World, 1967

Bleifeld, M., *Modern Biology in Review*, Barron's, 1969 (revised edition).

de Bono, E., *The Machanism of Mind*, Simon & Schuster, 1969.

Burns, G. W., *The Science of Genetics; An Introduction to Heredity*, Macmillan, 1969.

Calder, N., ed., *The World in 1984*, Pelican Books, 1965 (paperback, 2 vols.).

Calvin, M., *Chemical Evolution*, Oxford University Press, 1969.

Caullery, M., *A History of Biology*, Walker, 1966.

Clarke, A. C., *Profiles of the Future*, Harper & Row, 1963.

Committee on Government Operations, United States Senate, *Research in the Service of Man: Biomedical Knowledge, Development and Use*, U.S. Government Printing Office, 1967.

Cote, A. J., Jr., *The Search for the Robots*, Basic Books, 1967.

Daedalus (special issue), *Evolution and Man's Progress*, Summer 1961.

DeBusk, A. G., *Molecular Genetics*, Macmillan, 1968.

Delgado, J. M. R., *Physical Control of the Mind*, Harper & Row, 1969.

Ettinger, R. C. W., *The Prospect of Immortality*, Doubleday, 1964 (revised and updated paperback edition; Macfadden, 1966).

Firsoff, V. A., *Life Mind and Galaxies*, Oliver and Boyd, 1967.

Fishlock, D., *Man Modified: An Exploration of the Man/Machine Relationship*, Funk & Wagnalls, 1969.

Gamow, G., and Yčas, M., *Mr. Tompkins Inside Himself; Adventures in the New Biology*, Viking, 1967.

Good, I. J., *The Scientist Speculates; An Anthology of Partly-Baked Ideas*, Basic Books, 1962.

Guillerme, J., *Longevity*, Walker, 1963.

Halacy, D. S., Jr., *Bionics: The Science of "Living" Machines*, Holiday House, 1965.

————, *Radiation, Magnetism and Living Things*, Holiday House, 1966.

Handler, P., ed., *Biology and the Future of Man*, Oxford University Press, 1970.

Harris, H., *Nucleus and Cytoplasm*, Clarendon Press, 1968.

Harrison, G. R., *What Man May Be. The Human Side of Science*, Morrow, 1956.

Huxley, A., *Brave New World*, Harper & Bros., 1932, 1946.

————, *Brave New World Revisited*, Harper & Bros., 1958.

Johnson, E. G., and W. R. Corliss, *Teleoperators and Human Augmentation*, NASA/U.S. Government Printing Office, 1967.

Kavaler, L., *Freezing Point: Cold as a Matter of Life and Death*, Day, 1970.

Kenyon, D. H., and Steinman, G., *Biochemical Predestination*, McGraw-Hill, 1969.

Bibliography

Landers, R. R., *Man's Place in the Dybosphere*, Prentice-Hall, 1966.

Laycock, G., *The Alien Animals*, Natural History Press, 1966.

Lessing, L., *DNA: At the Core of Life Itself*, Macmillan, 1966, 67.

London, P., *Behavior Control*, Harper & Row, 1969.

McCusick, V. A., *Human Genetics*, 2nd ed., Prentice-Hall, 1969.

McHale, J., *Toward the Future*, Design Quarterly 72 (special issue), 1968.

Marteka, V., *Bionics*, Lippincott, 1965.

Medawar, P. B., *The Future of Man*, Basic Books, 1959.

National Academy of Sciences, *The Scientific Endeavor* (Centennial Celebration of the National Academy of Sciences), Rockefeller Institute Press, 1965.

Oparin, A. I., *Genesis, Evolutionary Development of Life*, (trans. from 1966 Russian ed.), Academic Press, 1968.

———, *Life: Its Nature, Origin and Development*, Academic Press, 1964.

Osborn, F., *The Future of Human Heredity*, Weybright & Talley, 1968.

Pickens, K., *Eugenics and the Progressives*, Vanderbilt University Press, 1968.

Portmann, A., *New Paths in Biology*, Harper & Row, 1963.

Prehoda, R. W., *Suspended Animation: The Research Possibility That May Allow Man to Conquer the Limiting Chains of Time*, Chilton, 1969.

Rinkel, M., ed., *Biological Treatment of Mental Illness*, L. C. Page, 1966.

Rosenblueth, A., *Mind and Brain: A Philosophy of Science*, M.I.T. Press, 1970.

Rosenfeld, A., *The Second Genesis: The Coming Control of Life*, Prentice-Hall, 1969.

Roslansky, J. D., ed., *Genetics and the Future of Man*, North Holland Press, 1966.

Schrödinger, E., *Mind and Matter*, Cambridge University Press, 1959.

———, *What Is Life?*, Cambridge University Press, 1962.

Silverstein, A., and V. B., *Germ Free Life: A New Field in Biological Research*, Lothrop, Lee & Shepard, 1970.

Simpson, G. G., *Biology and Man*, Harcourt, Brace & World, 1969.

Sonneborn, T. M., ed., *The Control of Human Heredity and Evolution*, Macmillan, 1965.

Stent, G. S., *The Coming of the Golden Age: A View of the End of Progress*, Natural History Press, 1969.

Still, H,. *Man: The Next Thirty Years*, Hawthorn, 1968.

Taylor, G. R., *The Biological Time Bomb*, World, 1968.

Teilhard de Chardin, P., *The Future of Man*, Harper & Row, 1964.

Thomson, G., *The Foreseeable Future*, Cambridge University Press, 1955.

Thompson, P. D., *A biogenesis: From Molecules to Cells*, Lippincott, 1969.

U.S. Department of Health, Education and Welfare, *Research Advances in Human Transplantation*, U.S. Government Printing Office, 1969.

Wall Street Journal, Here Comes Tomorrow, Dow-Jones Books, 1966 and 1967.

Warshofsky, F., *The Control of Life: The Twenty-first Century*, Viking, 1969.

Watson, J. D., *The Double Helix*, Atheneum, 1968.

Wells, H. G., et al., *The Science of Life*, Garden City Publishing Co., Inc., 1939.

Wolstenholme, G., ed., *Man and His Future*, Little, Brown, 1963.

Wooldridge, D. E., *The Machinery of Life*, McGraw-Hill, 1966.

———, *Mechanical Man, The Physical Basis of Intelligent Life*, McGraw-Hill, 1968.

Young, J. Z., and Margerison, T., eds., *The Explosion of Science, From Molecule to Man*, Crown, 1969.

ARTICLES

Anderson, John, "The Click of Computerized Medicine," *The UNESCO Courier*, March 1968.

Apgar, V., and Stickle, G., "Birth Defects," *Journal of the American Medical Association*, April 29, 1968.

Asimov, I., "The Perfect Machine," *Science Journal*, October 1968.

———, "Pills to Help Us Remember?," *New York Times Magazine*, October 9, 1966.

Atlantic Monthly, "Further Thoughts on the Biological Revolution," March 1969.

Bacq, Z. M., "A Viscious Circle of Chemicals Against Chemicals," in *The World of 1984*, N. Calder, ed., vol. 2.

Block, V., "Tomorrow's New Foods," *Science Digest*, January, 1967.

Brachet, J. (interviewed). "Beyond DNA," *Réalités*, March 1969.

Britten, R. J., and Kohne, D. E., "Repeated Segments of DNA," *Scientific American*, April 1970.

Burch, Philip, "Of Growth and Disease," *New Scientist*, November 28, 1968.

Campbell, L., "Clues from a Chemical," *Science News*, October 3, 1970 (re chemistry of the brain).

Carpenter, D. G., and Wrobel, J. E., Jr., "Is Biological Aging Inevitable?," *Analog*, December 1969.

Chargaff, E., "The Paradox of Biochemistry," *Columbia Forum*, Summer 1969.

Chase, S. S., "Anti-Famine Strategy: Genetic Engineering for Food," *Bulletin of the Atomic Scientists*, October 1969.

Comfort, Alex, "The Life Span of Animals," *Scientific American*, August 1961.

Corey, E. J., and Wipke, W. T., "Computer-Assisted Design of Complex Organic Syntheses," *Science*, October 10, 1969.

Cote, A. J., Jr., "Synthetic Nerves: Pathways to Artificial Intelligence," *Industrial Research*, May 1968.

Culliton, B. J., "Era of Plastic Hearts," *Science News*, April 11, 1970.

———, "Watching the Unborn," *Science News*, July 5, 1969.

Crow, J. F., "Mechanisms and Trends in Human Evolution," *Daedalus*, Summer 1961.

Delbrück, M., "A Physicist's Renewed Look at Biology: Twenty Years Later," *Science*, June 12, 1970.

DiCara, L. V., "Learning in the Autonomic Nervous System," *Scientific American*, January 1970.

Dobzhansky, T., "Changing Man," *Science*, January 27, 1967.

Dulbecco, R., "Cell Transformation by Viruses," *Science*, November 21, 1969.

Eisenberg, L., "Genetics and the Survival of the Unfit," *Harper's*, February 1966.

179

Bibliography

Englebart, D. C. (interviewed), "Augmenting Your Intellect," *Research/Development,* August 1968.

Fallaci, O., "The Dead Body and the Living Brain," *Look,* November 28, 1967.

Fleming, D., "On Living in a Biological Revolution," *Atlantic Monthly,* February 1969.

Ford, A. B., "Casualties of Our Time," *Science,* January 16, 1970.

Ford, B., "My Machine Loves Me," *Science Digest,* September 1970.

———, "Redesign Your Body: What Changes Would You Make?," *Science Digest,* November 1969.

Fourastié, J., "A Look at World Population the Day After Tomorrow," *The UNESCO Courier,* February 1967.

Frazier, K., "More Ways Than One to Kill a Bug," *Science News,* October 11, 1969.

Frisch, B., "Aging, the Disease with a Cure," *Science Digest,* February 1969.

Gardner, A. R., "Chemicals and Crustaceans: New Computer Routes," *Product Engineering,* March 4, 1963.

Garen, A., "Sense and Nonsense in the Genetic Code," *Science,* April 12, 1968.

German, J., "Studying Human Chromosomes Today," *American Scientist,* March–April 1970.

Gilman, W., "Tampering with the Genetic Blueprint," *New Republic,* November 22, 1966.

Harker, D., "The Molecules of Molecular Biology," *Physics Today,* August 1969.

Hayflick, L., "Human Cells and Aging," *Scientific American,* March 1968.

Hess, G. L., "Origins of Molecular Biology," *Science,* May 8, 1970.

Heston, L. L., "The Genetics of Schizophrenic and Schizoid Disease," *Science,* January 16, 1970.

Keeping, G. G., "Implantable Instrumentation," *Industrial Research,* April 1967.

Kolin, A., "Magnetic Fields in Biology," *Physics Today,* November 1968.

Kornberg, A., "The Synthesis of DNA," *Scientific American,* October 1968.

Krech, D., "The Chemistry of Learning," *Saturday Review,* January 20, 1968.

Lasagna, L., "The Pharmaceutical Revolution: Its Impact on Science and Society," *Science,* December 5, 1969.

Lasker, G. W., "Human Biological Adaptivity," *Science,* December 19, 1969.

Lear J., "Spinning the Thread of Life," *Saturday Review,* April 5, 1969.

Lederberg, J., "Experimental Genetics and Human Evolution," Bulletin of the Atomic Scientists, October 1966.

Lessing, L., "Into the Core of Life Itself," *Fortune,* March 1966.

Luria, S. E., "Modern Biology: A Terrifying Power," *The Nation,* October 20, 1969.

———, "The Recognition of DNA in Bacteria," *Scientific American,* January 1970.

Mayr, E., "Biological Man and the Year 2000," *Daedalus,* Summer 1967.

Mazur, P., "Cryobiology: The Freezing of Biological Systems," *Science,* May 22, 1970.

Merrifield, R. B., "The Automatic Synthesis of Proteins," *Scientific American,* March 1968.

Miller, N. E., "Chemical Coding of Behavior in the Brain," *Science,* April 16, 1965.

Muller, H. J. "Life Forms on Other Worlds," in *The Coming of the Space Age*, A. C. Clarke, ed., Meredith Press, 1967.

———, "Should We Weaken or Strengthen Our Genetic Heritage?," *Daedalus*, Summer 1961.

National Academy of Sciences, "Symposium on Genetic Implications of Demographic Trends," *Proceedings of the National Academy of Sciences*, March 15, 1968.

Oakley, M., "Computer Analysis of Protein Evolution," *Scientific American*, July 1969.

Perlman, D., "The Search for the Memory Molecule," *New York Times Magazine*, July 7, 1968.

Phillips, D. C., "The Three-Dimensional Structure of an Enzyme Molecule," *Scientific American*, November 1966.

Prehoda, R. W., "Perennial Youth— A Foreseeable Reality?," *Industrial Research*, August 1966.

Ptashne, M., and Gilbert, W., "Genetic Repressors," *Scientific American*, June 1970.

Quarton, G. C., "Deliberate Efforts to Control Human Behavior and Modify Personality," *Daedalus*, Summer 1967.

Reinert, J., "Brain Control: Tomorrow's Curse or Blessing?," *Science Digest*, November 1969.

Rorvik, D. M., "Cloning: Asexual Human Reproduction?," *Science Digest*, November 1969.

———, "Making Men and Women Without Men and Women," *Esquire*, April 1969.

Rosenfeld, A., "The New Man: What Will He Be Like?," *Life*, October 1, 1965.

Rushmer, R. F., and Huntsman, L. L., "Biomedical Engineering," *Science*, February 6, 1970.

Rusk, H. A., "Solving the Mystery of Birth Defects," *Parents' Magazine*, November 1969.

The Sciences, "Man Revised," December 1969.

Shapiro, H. I., "What Man Will Be Like in 101,961 A.D.," *New York Times Magazine*, August 13, 1961.

Shock, N. W., The Physiology of Aging, *Scientific American*, January 1962.

Sonneborn, T. M., "H. J. Muller, Crusader for Human Betterment," *Science*, November 15, 1968.

Spencer, W. T., "They're Not Robots, They're Cyborgs," *New York Times Magazine*, December 14, 1969.

Stock, R. W., "The Mouse Stage of the New Biology," *New York Times Magazine*, December 21, 1969.

———, "Will the Baby Be Normal?" *New York Times Magazine*, March 23, 1969.

———, "The XYY and the Criminal," *New York Times Magazine*, October 20, 1968.

Stong, C. C., "Experiments in Generating the Constituents of Living Matter from Inorganic Substances," *Scientific American*, January 1970.

The UNESCO Courier, "Our Health Tomorrow" (special issue), March 1968.

Valentinuzzi, M., "A Survey of Theoretical Approaches to Magnetic Growth Inhibition," *American Journal of Medical Electronics*, First Quarter 1966.

van Gindertael, J. M., "Longer Life —Less Sickness," *The UNESCO Courier*, March 1968.

Verzár, F., "The Aging of Collogen," *Scientific American*, April 1963.

Wallace, R. L., et al., "Artificial Kidneys," *Industrial Research,* March 1969.

Weiss, P. A., "Whither Life Sciences?," *American Scientist,* March–April 1970.

Wick, G. L., "Molecular Biology: Moving Toward an Understanding of Genetic Control," *Science,* January 9, 1970.

Winter, R., "Fetology: Doctoring Unborn Babies," *Science Digest,* November 1969.

Wolff, E. (interviewed), "Embryology, One Foot in the Brave New World," *Réalités,* January 1969.

Zapol, W. M., et al., "Artificial Placenta: Two Days of Total Extrauterine Support of the Isolated Premature Lamb Fetus," *Science,* October 31, 1969.

BOOKLETS

Asimov, I., and Dobzhansky, T., *The Genetic Effects of Radiation,* U.S. Atomic Energy Commission, 1966.

Milne, L. J. and M., *Biological Frontiers,* Public Affairs Pamphlets, 1966.

National Society for Medical Research, *Unraveling the Mystery of Viruses,* April 1969.

Taviss, I., and Koivumaki, J., *Implications of Biomedical Technology* (Research Review No. 1), Harvard University, Fall 1968.

U.S. Department of Health, Education and Welfare, *Research Advances in Human Transplantation,* U.S. Government Printing Office, 1969.

Index

183

186

Picture Credits

The American Museum of Natural History 79; American Telephone and Telegraph 123; Applied Physics Laboratory Johns Hopkins University 121; Bell Telephone Laboratories 99; California Institute of Technology 94; Case Western Reserve/Engineering Design Center 124; Chase Limited/Gulton Industries 22; Raymond F. Chen, M.D., Ph.D., National Institutes of Health 59; Cornell Aeronautical Laboratory 119, 148; Dr. J. M. R. Delgado, Yale University School of Medicine 130, 131; Dr. D. C. Engelbart, Stanford Research Institute 149; Fortune Magazine, March 1966, 40; Dr. S. W. Fox, Institute of Molecular Evolution, University of Miami 91; General Electric Research and Development Center 118, 163; Goodyear Tire and Rubber Company 30; Hutchins Photography Inc., Belmont, Mass. 23; Industrial Research, August 1966, 68; Dr. A. K. Kleinschmidt, New York University and Scientific American, January 1970, 62; Professor E. A. Kline, Iowa State University 108; Redrawn from R. Lansford, Natural History, August-September, 1970, 102; Dr. L. MacHattie, Harvard University 15; Massachusetts General Hospital, Massachusetts Institute of Technology, Liberty Mutual Inc., and Harvard Medical School 126; Medtronic Inc. 125; Dr. Oscar L. Miller, Jr., Oak Ridge National Laboratory 46; The Mount Sinai Hospital of New York 173; Dr. Hermann J. Muller, Indiana University 105; National Institutes of Health, National Heart Institute 27; The Rockefeller Foundation 73, 106, 162; Rockefeller University 47, 48, 69; Dick Saunders for Honeywell Systems and Research Division 145; Redrawn from C. Singer, A Short History of Scientific Ideas, Oxford University Press, 1959, 82; Smith, Kline and French 61; Strong and Elwyn, Human Neuroanatomy, 1959, The Williams and Wilkins Co., Baltimore, and P. Handler, Biology and the Future of Man, Oxford University Press, 1970, 133; Redrawn from P. D. Thompson, Abiogenesis, J. B. Lippincott Co., 1969, 88; United States Department of Agriculture, Office of Information 167; University of California, Lawrence Radiation Laboratory 154; University of Utah 144; Dr. Dorothy Warburton, College of Physicians and Surgeons, Columbia University 56; Yerkes Regional Research Center, Emory University 155.